R. D. Bartlett and Patricia P. Bartlett

Turtles and Tortoises

Everything about Selection, Care, Nutrition,
Breeding, and Behavior

With 72 Color Photographs

Illustrations by Michele Earle-Bridges

© Copyright 1996 by Barron's Educational Series, Inc.

Library of Congress Catalog Card No. 96-11156

Library of Congress Cataloging-in-Publication Data

Bartlett, Richard D., 1938–.
    Turtles and tortoises : everything about selection, care, nutrition, breeding, and behavior / R. D. Bartlett and Patricia P. Bartlett ; illustrations by Michele Earle-Bridges.
        p.   cm.—(A complete pet owner's manual)
    Includes bibliographical references (p. 112) and index.
    ISBN 0-8120-9712-2
    1. Turtles as pets. I. Bartlett, Patricia Pope, 1949– . II. Title. III. Series.
SF459.T8B37   1996
639.3′92—dc20   96-11156
                                               CIP

Printed in Hong Kong

98765432

About the Authors

R. D. Bartlett is a herpetologist who has authored more than 400 articles and three books, and coauthored an additional seven books. He lectures extensively and has participated in field studies across North and Latin America. In 1978 he began the Reptilian Breeding and Research Institute, a private facility. Since its inception, more than 150 species of reptiles and amphibians have been bred at RBRI, some for the first time in the United States under captive conditions. Successes at the RBRI include several endangered species.

R. D. Bartlett is a member of numerous herpetological and conservation organizations, a cohost on an on-line reptile and amphibian forum, and a contributing editor of *Reptiles* magazine.

Patricia Bartlett is a biologist and historian who has authored five books and coauthored seven books. A museum administrator for the last fifteen years, she has worked in both history and science museums. She received the America Public Works Association Heritage Award in 1985 and serves in numerous local and state organizations.

Photo Credits

J. H. Harding: Pages 86, 87, 96 top and bottom. All other photographs were taken by R. D. Bartlett.

Important Notes

Caution should be exercised before using any of the electrical equipment described in this book.

While handling turtles and tortoises you may occasionally receive bites or scratches. If your skin is broken, see your physician immediately.

Some terrarium plants may be harmful to the skin or mucous membranes of human beings. If you notice any signs of irritation, wash the area thoroughly. See your physician if the condition persists.

Turtles and tortoises may transmit certain infections to humans. Always wash your hands carefully after handling your specimens. Always supervise children who wish to observe your turtles and/or tortoises.

Contents

Albino turtles are of great interest to hobbyists. This is an albino hatchling Florida soft-shelled turtle, Trionyx ferox.

Acknowledgments

To Bill Love and Rob MacInnes of Glades Herp and Chris McQuade of Gulf Coast Reptiles (all of Ft. Myers, FL) we owe a debt of gratitude for allowing us to photograph many common and uncommon turtles and tortoises. Doug Foster of Hogtown Herps (Gainesville, FL) has provided us similar opportunities. Thanks are due Andy Highfield (Tortoise Trust, England) for allowing us to report his newly developed technique of oral worming and to Rich Funk, DVM (Brandon, FL) for providing us with the medication chart. Jim Harding (Okemos, MI) has provided us with slides and much information regarding the worsening plight of the American pond turtles in their natural habitats. We wish also to express appreciation to Tom Tyning (Pittsfield, MA) and Carl May (Lake Worth, FL) for companionship in the field. Lastly, we offer thanks to Bob and Ellen Nicol, turtle breeders in Anthony, FL, for both information and additional photographic opportunities.

Introduction

Making the Decision

How does one get started in keeping turtles and tortoises? Many of us began by keeping tropical fish. With tropical fish, it's a logical progression to try "just one" small turtle. After all, how much trouble could a little turtle be? And small turtles are so appealing!

So the first turtle is acquired and does well (although some of your fish seem to be missing), and before you know it you've decided to get another turtle. Two won't be any additional work, and will provide twice the wide-eyed charm.

From that point on, the hobby grows—more turtles (which equate to fewer fish)—and eventually you've added a land enclosure for a tortoise or two.

But there is more to successful keeping of turtles and tortoises in captivity than most of us suspect. To truly succeed with these shelled reptiles it is necessary to know the species involved and to understand the natural history of each. Among the turtles are dwellers of quiet waters, of fast-moving rivers, of estuaries, and even of woods and fields. Tortoises need just enough water to slake their thirst. (Needless to say, one of these terrestrial species is not a proper candidate for life with your fish.)

Advantages and Disadvantages

Chelonians—a broad term that means both turtles and tortoises — don't require a lot of room or a yard to run in. If you rent, landlords generally don't object to these pets. Both turtles and tortoises are responsive pets with modest needs, especially compared to a warm-blooded animal such as a dog or cat. Your local grocery, pet, and hardware stores can supply everything you (and your pets) will need for housing, supplies, and food.

Cost: How much of an investment does it take to get started in turtle- or tortoise-keeping? It depends to a large extent on how much space you want to devote to the setup and how much you'd like to spend. Of course, you want and need caging that provides the best possible space for your pet at the most reasonable investment of time and money on your part. The best news is that getting started isn't prohibitively expensive.

A long-term pet: Once you're all set up, how long will your pet live? Properly maintained, it is not unusual for turtles or tortoises to live 20 years

A healthy chelonian has bright eyes and a firm shell. The young of all types have a large head for their size.

or more in captivity. Tortoises often live the longer, with 50 years not being unusual.

The Differences

The aquatic turtles have webbed toes and spend the majority of their time in the water. These include the basking turtles (here, "basking" means the turtles crawl out onto logs or rocks to sun themselves) of the family Emydidae, which are the sliders, the spotted turtles, the painted turtles, the cooters, and the map turtles. Most aquatic turtles are species of freshwater habitats, but a few are estuarine or brackish water forms. Included in this family are a few terrestrial species, the box and wood turtles.

The "nonbasking" aquatic turtles include the mud and musk turtles (family Kinosternidae); the snapping turtles (family Chelydridae), the soft-shelled turtles (family Trionychidae), and the side-necked turtles (families Chelidae and Pelomedusidae). These turtles often sun themselves by floating at the water's surface or atop a patch of floating weeds, rather than emerging from the water.

The tortoises are exclusively land-bound chelonians of the family Testudinidae. Generally, the tortoises have highly domed shells. A few, such as the pancake and hinge-back tortoises, have lower silhouettes. The forefeet of burrowing species may be flattened from back to front and spadelike, for digging. Collectively, tortoises are awkward swimmers at best and can easily drown if they accidentally stumble into water that is too deep for escape.

What This Book Covers

In this book we'll talk about the freshwater and terrestrial turtles and the tortoises commonly offered in the pet markets. We'll discuss these creatures' housing and food needs. We will also explain the legalities of keeping turtles and tortoises. As with other animals, the keeping of some turtles and tortoises is subject to legal restrictions that you as a responsible individual need to know.

Understanding Your Pet Turtle or Tortoise

What Does Your Pet Need?

Like any other living creature, your pet turtle or tortoise needs the three basics—food, water, and shelter. But these three categories mean different things to different types of turtles and tortoises. Let's look at ways you can understand your pet's needs and behavior.

Food

Food not only provides energy for immediate needs, but maintains the turtle's health and provides for future growth. As turtles get older, their dietary needs may change. Learn about your pet. For instance, many sliders begin their lives as omnivores, accepting and seeking out insects, worms, and crunchy bits of underwater vegetation or surface-floating plants like duckweed. This preference is reflected in captivity, as well as in the wild. Baby sliders will occasionally snack on tank vegetation or romaine lettuce as well as animal matter. As they mature, they'll become more vegetarian, dining primarily on your aquarium plants, floating leaves of romaine lettuce, or any other dark-green lettuce; do not feed iceberg lettuce, which doesn't offer enough nutrition for your pet. Occasionally you may still want to offer thawed frozen smelt, trout chow, or a pelleted turtle food. Tortoises are essentially vegetarians throughout their lives, but prefer a wide variety of vegetables and fruit, and the occasional change generally gets a good response. Land turtles such as box turtles generally don't change their dietary habits, continuing to feed upon earthworms, apples, romaine, and tomatoes, with a bit of softened kibble dog food once a week or so.

A turtle or tortoise that is hungry generally seems to be restless, and moves about its enclosure, nosing at objects it encounters. Unfortunately, a chelonian that has gone without proper food for too long becomes weakened and apathetic; food that is offered too late may not be recognized or eaten, even when placed in full view.

A basking turtle warms itself by sunning.

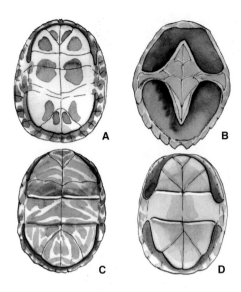

Although many chelonians have unremarkable plastrons like the basking turtles, (A), the lower shells of others such as the musk turtles (B), box turtles (C), and mud turtles (D) are distinctive.

Tortoises are characterized by unwebbed feet and highly domed shells.

Water

No matter what kind of chelonian you have, it needs water, if only to drink. Aquatic turtles will dehydrate, dessicate, and die if kept dry and allowed only enough water to drink. They need enough clean water to fully submerge and swim. Many kinds of aquatic turtles cannot swallow food unless they are submerged, no matter how hungry they may be.

Semiaquatic turtles need enough water to occasionally clamber in and become wet all over, although they do not need to be in water to eat. Their enclosures must be slightly more humid than those for the tortoises, and a "bathing-size" water dish will help keep the humidity high enough.

Tortoises and terrestrial turtles need a slightly smaller water dish, but these chelonians must always have clean water available to drink.

Shelter

Although chelonians thermoregulate by sunning, they seek places of seclusion when it comes time to sleep. If no area of seclusion is provided, tortoises will sleep, nose in, in a corner of their pen. Depending on the weather, our tortoises sleep under low-growing bushes in their enclosure or inside their tortoise house. Turtles often sleep submerged but clinging to vegetation or twigs, so that the surface is not more than a few inches away. Provide an area where they can sleep underwater and yet feel secluded. Semiaquatic turtles such as wood turtles will sleep under grass hummocks or burrowed into clumps of sphagnum.

Behavior Notes

Unlike many other reptiles such as snakes or iguanas that respond to an implied threat by biting or lashing with the tail, chelonians withdraw into their shells. They are generally quick to take fright. If possible, aquatic types simply

When given adequate substrate, several turtle species will construct home burrows. Here a bog turtle, Clemmys muhlenbergi, *peers from its "den."*

may swim away quickly. Once frightened into their shells, new captives are slow to emerge, and any fast movement on your part is apt to make them withdraw again. Chelonians are also sensitive to loud noises, vibrations, and sudden bright lights.

If the species involved have somewhat reduced shells (snapping and musk turtles) or otherwise modified shells (soft-shelled turtles and pancake tortoises), there has usually developed an alternate means of defense such as strong jaws and claws or increased agility. Chelonians that are ill tend to stay withdrawn in their shells, which makes not only diagnosis but treatment and feeding difficult. For more information on choosing a healthy turtle or tortoise, see the next chapter. For information on treating a turtle or tortoise that is ill, see Health and Medications on page 32.

Choosing a Healthy Turtle or Tortoise

What to Look For

Turtles and tortoises are well known for their habit of withdrawing into their shell and remaining so for long periods. Wild specimens are more apt to do this than captive-bred ones; wild-collected adults are especially prone to withdrawing their head, limbs, and tail from sight. Tortoises are often even more retiring than turtles. This habit may make assessing the health of a given specimen difficult—especially for a novice.

What should you look for when considering the purchase of a turtle or tortoise? How does the appearance of a healthy specimen differ from that of one that is ill? And, if the specimen does withdraw, what then?

All things, *including* the agility with which the animal withdraws its soft parts and the persistence with which it remains hidden must be considered when choosing a turtle or tortoise. There *are* a couple of things that you can consider even when it is withdrawn, and there is a nonthreatening trick or two that you can use to induce the turtle or tortoise to cooperate.

First, *slowly* approach the specimen in which you are interested. To a chelonian that is already frightened by capture and caging, the presence of any large approaching shape implies danger, and a fast-moving large shape is usually considered more dangerous than a slow-moving or stationary one. If you move slowly you may be able to approach rather closely without inducing a complete withdrawal by the spec-

imen. If the turtle is a type normally associated with water, it is less likely to withdraw fully if it is submerged than if it is out of water. Once touched, a frightened turtle will remain withdrawn longer than if not touched.

Eyes: If you are able to see the turtle's or tortoise's eyes, are they bright and clear? They should be—even if the turtle is beneath the water's surface. If out of water, the turtle's eyes should have neither exudate nor encrustations around or beneath them, nor should the eyelids be puffy and swollen. Does the animal follow your movements with its eyes? It should.

Breathing: There should be no bubbling or wheezing from the nostrils, even when the head is quickly withdrawn. Either of these manifestations probably indicates a respiratory ailment. The turtle/tortoise should be breathing normally (through its nostrils with mouth closed) rather than gasping with an open mouth. Open-mouth breathing indicates nasal passage obstructions. These are most often associated with a respiratory ailment.

Swimming: If in the water, does the turtle submerge easily and fully and retain an even keel when submerged and swimming? Or, does the turtle float like a cork with one side higher than the other? If your answer is yes to the first question and no to the second one, all is probably well. If you have answered no to the first part and/or yes to the second, the specimen in question may have problems. Respiratory distress can result in the specimen's swimming on an uneven keel or bobbing on the surface and failing to submerge. Do not purchase the specimen.

For an aquatic species, when it is in the water, check the turtle to assure that it does not have open wounds or fungus-covered bruises on its soft parts. Although most external fungi are easily eradicated, there is no reason to start out with a problem. Fungus may appear either as a fuzzy cottony growth or as a rather smooth, velvety sheet. Do not confuse fungal infections (white chlorophyll-free growths) with algal growths. The latter are usually green and grow on the shell (more rarely the limbs) of highly aquatic turtle species. Algal growths are harmless.

Lift the turtle or tortoise. Unless it is a soft-shelled turtle or a pancake tortoise, its shell should be firm (hatchlings) to rigid (adults). The shells of soft-shelled turtles (*Trionyx* species) and the pancake tortoise (*Malacochersus tornieri*) are naturally softer and more pliable than the shells of other turtle and tortoise species. The shells of the hatchlings of all species are somewhat less firm than those of older specimens.

All limbs should be fully functional and not swollen. When the chelonian is lifted, do its legs dangle limply from the shell or are they easily straightened when gently pulled? A yes answer to either question likely indicates a problem—possibly malnutrition. Advanced problems can vary from difficult to impossible to correct. Do not purchase the specimen.

Shell: Does the shell have cracks, breaks, missing scutes, or is it pitted? At best your answers will be no, no, no, and no. But some chelonians do experience the trauma of shell breaks or forest fires in the wild. Cracks and breaks can occur and heal satisfactorily (resulting only in cosmetic disfigurement once completely healed).

Burns that have resulted in the loss of scutes may heal and scar—again only a cosmetic problem. If the animal is otherwise healthy and you do not mind the unnatural appearance, there is no reason that you should not purchase it. While the pitting may result from some natural cause, it is most often seen on captives that have been maintained in unclean or other unsuitable conditions. Like shell breaks, if the pitting is old and well healed, it should cause no further problems. If the pits are unclean and contain an odorous, caseous (cheeselike) material, the problem is active and the specimen should be shunned.

It is often necessary to play a waiting game when you wish to get a good look at a shy tortoise. These creatures are very adept at retiring into their shell, folding their forelimbs tightly in front of their head, and sitting for very long periods without displaying any animation. When they finally decide to check things out, they often do so by relaxing the forelimbs somewhat, peering out from between folded elbows, and withdrawing again at the slightest motion. Attempting to check a recalcitrant tortoise can be a true exercise in futility.

What to beware of:
Do not purchase a turtle or tortoise with the following conditions:
• Open, unhealed breaks or cracks in the shell
• Pits in its shell that contain a caseous, usually odorous, material
• Shell of a hatchling not firm; shell of an adult not rigid
• Listless mien
• Swollen eyelids
• Swollen limbs
• Exudate around or beneath the eyes
• Bubbles from the nostrils when breathing or exudate around the nostrils
• Open-mouth breathing

Although sexual characteristics will be mentioned in the various species accounts, here are a few generalities. All pertain to specimens approaching sexual maturity.

The **plastron** (bottom shell) of the males of some turtle and tortoise species is indented (concave). This appears more frequently on terrestrial turtles and tortoises. The concavity allows the male to initially assume a better breeding stance. The concavity does not occur in many semiaquatic turtles, the breeding postures of which are buoyed by the water.

The **foreclaws** of the males of certain semiaquatic turtles are greatly lengthened. Among the species so adorned are the sliders, cooters, painted turtles, and map turtles.

The **tails** of male turtles and tortoises are longer and thicker than those of the females. The vent opening of a male is also positioned more distally from the rear edge of the plastron than that of the female.

• Swimming with one side higher than the other (if a water species)
• Difficulty submerging (if a water species)
• Limbs that dangle weakly or are easily straightened when the animal is lifted
• Limbs obviously flaccid and thin

Trouble signs: If, after getting a chelonian home, it develops any of the described symptoms, immediately consult both the health section of this book (page 32) and a veterinarian who is qualified to treat reptile/amphibian ailments and diseases. Respiratory disease can be communicable and can be caused by a number of different pathogens. Not all of the pathogens respond to the same antibiotics. Isolate any turtle or tortoise that shows symptoms of respiratory distress and have sensitivity tests performed.

Always remember that chelonians can be hosts of *Salmonella*. **Wash your hands before and after handling *any* turtles or tortoises** (but most especially if the specimen is in dirty water).

Ask to see the animal eat. Most *healthy* chelonians have fine appetites. A very few specimens may outwardly appear healthy, but refuse to feed. Often this lack of appetite results from either illness or an improper diet being offered. It is always a good idea to see the animal feed. Most aquatic turtles prefer to feed in the water. Some well-acclimated specimens will accept food while out of the water, but will nearly invariably return to the water to consume their morsels. Swallowing is eased by the presence of water in the turtle's mouth and throat. Some hobbyists feel that many aquatic turtle species are unable to swallow unless they *are* underwater. Although many of our specimens can and do eat when out of water, most *prefer* to feed while in water.

A healthy turtle or tortoise eagerly feeds on offered food.

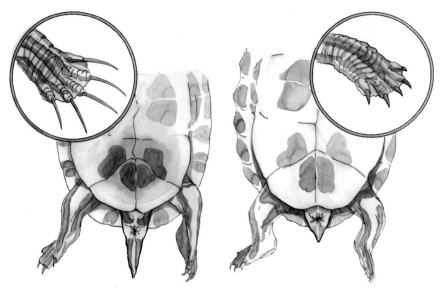

All aquatic turtles can be sexed by the location of the vent in relation to the edge of the carapace and some by the length of the claws on the front feet. A male has the vent near the edge of the carapace; some types also have long front claws. A female has the vent inside the edge of the carapace and short claws.

Male or Female?

Truthfully, unless you intend to breed your turtles and tortoises, the sex of a specimen is unimportant. Both males and females of most species make equally good pets. The males of some species are larger than the females. In other cases either the opposite is true or both sexes attain a similar size. Even if it *does* make a difference, it is nearly impossible to accurately sex hatchling and juvenile turtles and tortoises. It is only when the animals are approaching sexual maturity that the secondary characteristics that allow us to sex them by sight become obvious.

Where Should You Get Your Turtle or Tortoise?

There are many sources from which you may get a turtle or tortoise. You may choose to collect your own from the wild. Before doing so, check with the landowner if necessary and be sure to check your state's game and nongame laws. Many turtles are protected, some in all states in which they range, some only in the states where they are most uncommon. You may need authorization to collect or keep a native turtle or tortoise, or you may not be legally able to do so at all. Some endangered and threatened species require specific permits. Failure to obtain these is a more serious offense than you may think.

Many pet shops carry the more commonly available kinds of turtles and tortoises. Should you choose this avenue of acquisition and are not an experienced hobbyist, bring a knowledgeable person with you to help you assess the overall health of the specimen in which you are interested.

When your turtles are shipped via air freight, they will be sent in muslin bags packed within a wooden crate.

Specialty reptile dealers and turtle and tortoise breeders advertise regularly in the classified sections of hobbyist-oriented reptile and amphibian magazines. Most are honest and try to supply healthy specimens of high quality; some are unscrupulous. Check the reliability of a given company or person with fellow hobbyists. Since in most cases you will be purchasing the specimen without inspection or appraisal, it is a case of buyer beware. Ask pertinent and pointed questions about the appearance, health, and general hardiness of the specimen and species in question. Be aware that shipping charges (including COD fees if applicable) significantly increase the purchase price.

Do not expect every specimen, especially wild-collected ones, to look picture-book perfect. Turtles and tortoises may vary widely in ground color, markings, and even adult size. The time to ask questions is *before* the purchase, not *after*. Good luck!

Looking for a specific turtle or tortoise? Check the classified ads in hobbyist magazines.

Housing for Turtles and Tortoises

There are several easily set up and easily maintained caging types, depending on the type of turtle or tortoise you are keeping and your own needs.

Housing for Turtles

Most turtles need to be either in water or close to it, but some types, such as the wood turtle or the box turtle, are more terrestrial than aquatic. Whatever kind of turtle you have, remember to add a lamp or hot-spot (an incandescent bulb, usually 75 watts or more, which emits heat and light) over the basking area.

Aquatic Turtles

Indoor caging: You'll need an aquarium (remember, aquatic turtles are active, so the larger the tank, the better), 1 inch (2.5 cm) or so of river rock or gravel on the bottom, and a filter system. Filtration can be under-gravel or via an outside filter.

If you use an undergravel filter, attach a powerhead pump or a small vibrator-type aerating pump to the upright filter tube. The powerhead pump provides a fairly strong water current that pulls down and filters the water through the gravel and then pushes the water out the top of the powerhead. The small vibrator-type pump does the same with reduced power by using air bubbles to push water through the upright filter tube. Keep in mind that turtles that are weak swimmers or small turtles may not be able to swim comfortably against the stronger current caused by the powerhead.

Add large *smooth* rocks or semisubmerged logs for a haul-out area under the tank's light or hot-spot. Your basking turtles, the sliders and cooters, will avail themselves of a dry haul-out and spend a good part of the day sunning. If you have tiny hatchling turtles that you've caught yourself (you cannot legally buy any turtles that are less than 4 inches (10 cm) long, because of *Salmonella* concerns), a good-sized patch of floating aquatic plants will work for a resting/sunning area. Musk and soft-shelled turtles will rest atop these floating plants, rather than on a log or rock.

Place the tank on a sturdy tabletop or on a stand and pour in the rinsed river rock or gravel. Spread the rock or gravel evenly. We prefer river rock

Glass terrariums can be easily cleaned with a weak bleach solution and paper towels.

Small aquatic turtles do well in a simple aquarium set up with a filter, incandescent lighting, and a haul-out area. Undergravel filters can be used together with outside filters to help keep the water clean.

The smooth river rock used in aquariums makes a good substrate for aquatic turtles.

Many aquatic turtle species are at home in deep aquariums. Among other species, this tank houses Siebenrock's snake-necked turtles, Chelodina siebenrocki.

because the stones are rounded, not sharp like aquarium gravel. Turtles routinely search along the bottom of their tank and ingest gravel as part of the feed/exploration process. If too much sharp gravel is ingested, intestinal impaction can occur.

Add water to about half the depth of the tank. If you're keeping soft-shelled turtles, you may want to add a dechlorinator to remove the chlorine from the water. Soft-shelled turtles have a leathery, soft shell rather than the hard shells of most turtles, and so are more subject to shell damage and fungus problems (especially as babies—and *most* especially, the babies of the Florida soft-shelled turtle, *Trionyx ferox*).

If you add plants to your tank, almost any type of aquatic plant can be used. Plants add to the appearance of the tank; turtles may use them as resting areas and munch on them as well. Plants netted "out of the wild" may bear the additional bonus of tiny succulent insects and snails. Be prepared to add more plants as the old ones are eaten. You'll need to replant them in the tank when they are uprooted by the turtles. Place your plants, rocks, and logs to advantage.

Being air-breathers, of course, turtles need to be able to stick their noses above the surface of the water. A lower water level—one about 5 inches (12.5 cm) or less—means the turtles can draw a fresh breath of air while standing on the bottom of the tank, simply by standing on their toes and extending their necks. A lower water level also makes it easier for the turtles to crawl out on their haul-out areas to dry off, and eliminates the possibility of their getting too close to the overhead light or crawling out of the tank altogether. If you want to fill your tank nearer to the top, be certain that there are floating logs so your turtles can crawl out, dry off, and sun themselves under the aquarium light.

Semiterrestrial Turtles

Turtles that are well adapted to spending part of their life on land are called semiterrestrial turtles. Two examples are wood turtles and box turtles. Enclosures for the semiterrestrials need more land than water. The land base is created by placing 1 to 2 inches (2.5–5 cm) of river gravel in the bottom of a tank, placing a layer of nylon netting or air conditioner filtering material atop the gravel, and then adding 1 to 2 inches (2.5–5 cm) of potting soil on top. The netting or filtration material prevents the topsoil from shifting into the gravel, while the gravel serves as a drainage reservoir that keeps the topsoil damp without becoming soggy.

The substrate for woodland semiterrestrial turtles can be air conditioning filtration material between the topsoil and river rock gravel.

Water for these terrestrials can be provided in a dish that is firmly anchored in the substrate. The dish needs to be large enough for a turtle to drink from and crawl into, but not so deep that the turtle cannot crawl out of it. This water will need to be kept clean by frequent changes; although semiterrestrial turtles do not need to defecate into water, many seem to prefer it. The water will also get dirty from the bits of soil clinging to the turtle's face or shell. Changing the water three or four times a week should be sufficient.

Like the aquatic turtles, the semiterrestrial turtles will be more comfortable if they have a hiding place. This can be a box with an entry hole, a piece of flat bark placed over the rims of two adjacent small pots of plants, or any other type of enclosing space. However, some specimens may merely wedge themselves tightly into a corner of the enclosure, using this in preference to the enclosure you have provided. Many terrestrial turtles (and tortoises, too) will return to the same spot each night to sleep.

The enclosure for the wood and box turtles lends itself well to additional decoration in the form of plants or artistically shaped logs. Plants can stay in their pots and simply be embedded in the substrate up to the pot rims. (Since semiterrestrial turtles are, by nature, rather like small bulldozers, the plants used should be

Caging for some turtles, such as the Asian big-headed turtle, Platysternon megacephalum, *shown here, can be extremely simple.*

sturdy, nontoxic if nibbled, able to withstand substantial abuse, and/or readily replaced.) Vines, like philodendron, lend themselves to this sort of tank, and their stems provide more exploration areas for the turtles. The semiterrestrial turtles, which tend to be more adventuresome and active than either the wholly aquatic turtles or the tortoises, will investigate any new addition to their enclosure.

Housing for Tortoises

Tortoises need almost the same type of enclosure as the semiterrestrials, but prefer even drier conditions. Substrate for them can be dry river rock, newspaper, mulch, pieces of indoor-outdoor carpeting cut to the size of the enclosure, or the tiny compressed alfalfa pellets used as rabbit food. Each type of substrate, of course, has its advantages and disadvantages.

River rock is easy to wash when dirty and provides traction that makes walking easy.

Newspaper is readily available, absorbent, and easily changed, but its smooth surface makes walking uncomfortable if not actually difficult for most

Alfalfa pellets can be used as an absorbent substrate for tortoises or terrestrial turtles, but must be changed frequently.

tortoises. We use newspaper only short-term, such as during transport.

Cypress or pine mulch (never cedar; it contains phenols that are harmful to skin and lungs of reptiles) provides good footing and is absorbent.

Indoor-outdoor carpeting also provides a secure walking surface and can be washed or discarded when it becomes dirty.

Pelleted alfalfa is dry, inexpensive, and provides traction, and if it's accidentally ingested while the tortoise is feeding, no harm is done. However, since the pellets absorb both moisture and contaminants, the condition of the alfalfa pellets must be carefully monitored.

Provide water in a shallow, untippable container. We have used stainless steel water dishes that are square and can be wedged against a corner of the cage, as well as larger ceramic dog watering bowls. We have also used small plastic dishes, partially buried in the substrate, and have reconciled ourselves to straightening and refilling them more frequently than the heavier dishes and to changing the substrate more frequently to keep it dry.

In the wild, tortoises have a rather well-defined home range and usually a shelter (of sorts) to which they regularly retire. Captives should be provided with a hiding place much like that provided for the semiterrestrial turtles. A cardboard box with an access hole works well, or if you add a few pots of vines and pull some of the twining stems to one side, the tortoise may use the vines as cover.

Light and Heat

You'll need to provide a source of heat and light for turtles and tortoises. Like most of us, most turtles and tortoises prefer bright light. For them a bright light activates feeding and other activity responses. Combined light and heat is especially important during the cooler months.

A tortoise terrarium set-up must provide a hiding place, a hot-spot, a feeding area, water, and a substrate that offers walking traction.

18

The light and heat are important because chelonians are dependent on external heat sources; if they can't warm up, body functions (such as digestion) slow or stop. A warm turtle or tortoise feeds readily, is able to digest its food, and is alert enough to respond to your presence. Depending on its area of origin, a chelonian will be most comfortable when kept from 75 to 85°F (24–29°C), with a hot-spot basking area.

There are a couple of easy ways to heat your chelonian's enclosure. For aquatic turtles, you can use a submersible aquarium heater, one that lies on the bottom of the tank. (With a lowered tank level, the usual hang-over-the-edge heaters cannot be used.) If you choose an in-tank heater, protect it from being banged against the side of the tank by the turtles as they explore and feed. Some people use an electric heating pad underneath the tank, being sure the pad and its wire always are protected from the water in the tank.

An under-tank heater (a specially made heating "pad") will fit underneath an aquatic tank or under a terrarium and so is safe from being damaged by an active turtle or tortoise.

Even if under-tank heaters are used, brilliantly illuminated basking areas will be appreciated by your turtles and tortoises. For an aquatic tank, center the illumination above the haul-out area. Remember that fluorescent fixtures provide light but little heat. We use a 75-watt incandescent bulb in a round metal reflector, suspended over the tank about 12 to 18 inches (30–45 cm) above the basking/haul-out area. Temperature on the basking area should be about 88 to 94°F (31–34°C); the water in the tank must be cooler for thermoregulation.

This type of incandescent light will also work for your tortoises, again centered over the spot in the enclosure that is the hot-spot. For both turtles and tortoises, provide at least six hours of warmth-with-light a day.

Incandescent lights, like the standard fluorescent light, do not provide full-spectrum lighting. There are now both incandescent and fluorescent bulbs that are said to provide full-spectrum lighting, but read the label to see what type of ultraviolet (UV) rays are emitted by the bulb.

The term "full-spectrum lighting," as used here, indicates bulbs that emit light of approximately the color of natural sunlight, including UV-A and UV-B rays. At the moment, it appears that only certain fluorescent bulbs can fill the bill. Despite being sold as "full-spectrum" by their manufacturers, it seems that incandescent bulbs currently available do not emit the beneficial UV rays. Present-day incandescent bulbs would be better termed "color-corrected" than full-spectrum. You may wish to provide full-spectrum lighting for your pets on the theory that it can't hurt, but the truth seems to be that

For inside tortoises, an untippable water dish prevents spills.

Choose among these techniques to heat an aquatic cage: overhead incandescent light, submerged aquarium heater, or under-tank heating pad. The fluorescent light in the hood provides illumination only, not an appreciable amount of heat.

full-spectrum lighting isn't an absolute necessity when maintaining most chelonians. However, since UV-A and UV-B rays assist reptiles in synthesizing and metabolizing certain vitamins and minerals, if full-spectrum lighting is not utilized, vitamin D_3 and calcium supplements must be provided regularly. Although some successful turtle keepers/breeders do not supply full-spectrum lighting, we tend to be more comfortable hedging our bets, as the saying goes, and when our turtles and tortoises spend more than a month indoors, we provide full-spectrum lighting via the "full spec" fluorescent bulbs.

Outdoor Caging

Outdoor caging not only decreases your workload, but provides a better environment for your turtles and tortoises. The length of time during the day/year that your turtles can be kept outside will be determined by both the temperature of the surrounding environment (ambient temperature) and the turtle/tortoise species involved. As may be expected, species from temperate regions can withstand cooler

A free-form pool, whether lined with plastic or concrete, can become the focal point for your backyard.

temperatures for longer periods than can tropical forms.

Aquatic turtles do quite well in something as simple as a kiddie wading pool. Buy one without a ramp leading to the rim of the pool, or your turtles may take advantage of the opportunity to do some real traveling.

Place the pool in a partially shaded area. The turtles need and enjoy sun, but the small amount of water in the pool will heat up quickly. Create sunning areas for the turtles by positioning logs and/or smooth rocks in the center of the pool, and add the water with a garden hose. (You can probably see already how much less work an outdoor enclosure is going to be; cleaning and refilling is easy.) Keep the water level high enough so the turtles can totally submerge, but not so deep that they can lever themselves over the edge of the pool. Add turtles, feed as needed, and clean the pool every couple of days or when needed. You can hose off the algae or wipe the pool down as part of the cleaning process; don't add any chemicals to kill or inhibit the algae. The only problem with this type of pool is that it provides no land area for the female to lay her eggs, and eggs laid in water will literally drown.

If you can devote any type of yard space to the aquatic turtle pond, you can submerge it to its rim in the soil, and add a 1-foot-high (30 cm) fence about 3 feet (91 cm) from the rim of the pond.

Plant shrubbery and other types of cover, especially if the pond receives more than a couple of hours of direct sun each day. This will enable your turtles to wander about at will on the dry land, and should a female be carrying eggs, she can easily dig a hole to bury her eggs.

Garden Pools

Turtle pools need not be merely of the child's wading variety. They may be as elaborate as you wish. A free-form pool that we constructed while in central Florida was about 20 feet (6 m) long and 12 feet (3.6 m) wide. We even built a little bridge over the pool and would sit for long periods observing the many turtles it contained. Its depth varied from about 18 inches (45 cm) at the deepest point to only some 12 inches (30 cm) at the shallow end. The pool was made of reinforced cement, troweled to a smooth finish to assure that the turtles did not abrade their plastra while entering or leaving the water.

A small, galvanized, livestock watering trough makes a sturdy pond for aquatic turtles. To avoid escapes, put the haul-out areas in the center.

We had far less elaborate pools while we were in southwestern Florida. They were merely galvanized cattle watering tanks that were 8 feet (2.4 m) in diameter. In these we maintained a water depth of about 18 inches (45 cm) and positioned some large pieces of driftwood and sunken logs for haul-out perches. In the pool that housed the basically nonherbivorous map turtles, we were even able to grow hardy water lilies as well as some plants that have submerged roots, thus enjoying both the activities of the turtles and the beauty of the plants.

The vegetation in the pool containing the sliders had to be tougher. The herbivorous preferences of these turtles restricted the growing plants to emergents such as St. Johnswort, cattails, and other nonpalatable species.

Both semiterrestrial turtles and tortoises do well if they're in a fenced enclosure with a sunken water dish. A Pyrex baking dish is sturdy enough to be hosed out or lifted and cleaned and yet shallow enough to allow the turtles to enter and leave at will. The lid of a trash container, sunk to its rim, may be a more suitable water container for multiple or larger specimens. You need to keep the water container fairly shallow because some of the semiterrestrial turtles, such as the box turtle, do not swim well. A plastic container lid

The lid of a galvanized garbage can works well as a shallow outdoor water dish.

21

Terrestrial turtles and tortoises that become overturned must right themselves before they overheat and die.

placed on the ground will keep food items out of the dirt. A hiding area such as a pile of leaf litter, planted shrubs, or a hiding box will provide your turtle or tortoise with a greater feeling of security.

Overheating: Tortoises and highly domed turtles are not agile, and they may overturn. Once overturned, they may find it difficult or impossible to right themselves. If this occurs in full sunlight or beneath a heat lamp, your pet may overheat and die. Although there is no fail-safe method to prevent this, you *must* take every precaution possible. Take stock of your caging, redecorate as prudent, and check your chelonian daily.

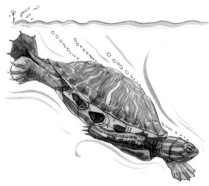

A turtle will plunge into water to cool off.

The Enclosed Garden

Although not often used by American hobbyists, the European concept of tortoises and terrestrial turtles wandering free in an enclosed garden or yard does find favor with some. Throughout the years our Aldabra giant and radiated tortoises have had full run of the fenced-in yard. They enjoy the space so provided and we enjoy a far greater degree of intimacy with the tortoises. In fact, all follow us around like so many well-trained dogs, moving if we move and gathering around us when we stop. If we reach down to scratch them, they stand high on tiptoes, necks stretched as far upward as possible. In this position they allow us—they actually seem to ask us—to scratch necks, legs, and even the top of their heads.

If you feed the turtles and tortoises in one place and at a particular time, the creatures will often gather daily in anticipation of their meal and they learn equally fast where their night house is. Even in southern Florida it was necessary to heat the night house on some of the colder evenings. This we accomplished by using red or blue heat lamps, neither of which seemed to disturb the tortoises' 24-hour biological cycle (circadian rhythms) and breeding cycles in the slightest.

We learned early on that no matter how tightly a steel-mesh fence is stretched, there is no such thing as tortoise-escape-proof chain-link fencing. Both the Aldabra and radiated tortoises can walk right under what seems to be a taut, ground-hugging chain-link fence. Reinforce the bottom of the fencing by securing ground-level rebars (reinforcing bars) parallel to the ground between the fenceposts. An alternative is to run treated 1 × 6s along the bottom of the fence, staking them at 4-foot (1.2 m) intervals.

In some areas of the country cinder block walls are commonly placed around yards and gardens. These are ideal for the chelonians and need no additional preparation at all.

About Laws on Keeping Turtles

A Special Caution about *Salmonella*

Many keepers of turtles and tortoises remember when baby turtles were offered for sale on the countertops of almost every variety store in America. Now turtles under 4 inches (10 cm) in length may be sold only to researchers.

Why is this so and how did it come to be?

Well, certainly for humane reasons changes were needed. But it was not the ethics of humane treatment that stopped baby turtle sales. Rather, it was concern about the possible spread of a bacterial disease—salmonellosis (often just referred to by the generic name of the bacterium—*Salmonella*).

Salmonella is an omnipresent bacterium, and improper hygiene in the tanks of baby turtles often assured that it would be present in noteworthy concentrations in those containers. Grasping the bull by the horns, so to speak, in the late 1970s, conservationists and health officials combined forces and a federal law was passed preventing the sale of baby turtles— of any turtle (including tortoises)— with a shell length of 4 inches (10 cm) or less. The rationale was that the toddlers for whom the baby turtles were often purchased as pets would be unable to put a turtle of 4-inch (10 cm) (or greater) size in their mouths; thus possible contamination by *Salmonella* bacteria would be lessened.

The fallacy, of course, is that though the turtles may not fit easily in the mouth, fingers do. If *Salmonella* are present, unwashed hands can easily transmit the bacteria to the mouth.

A determined tortoise can escape by wedging itself under the stretchable lower edge of chain-link fencing.

Thus, the bottom line here is to caution both adults and children: Turtles *can* carry diseases that are transmissible to humans, and *you* may inadvertently introduce pathogens to your pets if you handle them or offer them food without first washing your hands. If

Tortoises like the Madagascar radiated tortoise can become well socialized and enjoy being petted.

you wash your hands both before and following the handling of any pet turtles or tortoises, you will help protect both your pets and yourself.

Today, additional laws that affect the availability of turtles and tortoises in the pet trade have also been enacted. Because of plummeting turtle populations (caused by habitat and nest destruction and collecting for pet, food, and research markets), many states now fully or partially protect all or some indigenous turtle species. Endangered species regulations on state, federal, and international levels offer even greater protection to some species. Importation restrictions limit the availability of many foreign turtle species once sought by American hobbyists.

But despite all of the laws and regulations, people continue to keep turtles and tortoises, baby and otherwise. Many persons, like ourselves, are breeders of both common and unusual turtles and tortoises. Baby turtles are found by anglers who take them home to their families, children pick up box and wood turtles on woodland pathways, and there are reptile dealers that can supply a vast number of species. Specialty clubs, catering to cheloniophiles (turtle enthusiasts) are present in many large cities.

Thus, if you want a turtle, you can get a turtle. That many people not only do want a turtle but want to know more about it is shown by the many questions we field.

Feeding and Watering

Watering

Although many arid-land tortoises metabolize much of their moisture requirements from the food they eat, it is important that all captive chelonians be provided clean water at all times. Tortoises are not nimble creatures. Not only must the water dish be easy to drink from, but it must be shallow enough so the tortoise won't drown if it happens to bumble in and overturn.

Water receptacles may be small enough so that the tortoise/turtle only drinks from it, or large enough to allow your pet to fully enter and soak. Whatever the size, the receptacles must be shallow and they must be kept full. To protect the plastron from abrasion, the sides must be smooth and easily negotiated.

Aquatic chelonians will, of course, drink from their swimming water—another reason that filtration and changing is so important. Do note that many aquatic turtle species feed in the water. Depending on the number of turtles kept in any self-contained aquatic enclosure and the gallonage of the enclosure itself, occasional to frequent and partial to complete water changes should be routinely made.

Feeding

You have one simple goal in feeding your turtle or tortoise: learn what your pet eats in the wild and strive to simulate this. Your pet will be much the better for your efforts.

Here are some general guidelines. For species-specific suggestions, read the species accounts beginning on page 46. Keep in mind that you must stop feeding any chelonians you intend to hibernate two weeks (or more, depending on ambient temperatures) prior to placing them into hibernation. (See pages 43–45 on hibernation.)

Supplementation: In all diets, augment with calcium and multivitamins (specifically D_3 and some A). This is especially important in fast-growing hatchlings and juveniles and in ovulating females, all of which are actively metabolizing calcium.

For all reptiles, a diet with the correct calcium to phosphorus balance is important to maintain bone integrity. If the reptile does not receive enough calcium in its diet to maintain the correct level in the blood, the needed

Fruits and Vegetables with Calcium/Phosphorous Ratio of 1:1 or Better
avocado
beet greens
blackberries
blueberries
broccoli stem or leaf (not florets)
cabbage
Chinese cabbage
cantaloupe
carrots
cauliflower
celery
chard
collards
dandelion greens
endive
green beans
kohlrabi
okra

calcium is taken from the bones. The bones are softened and muscles weaken; the syndrome is termed metabolic bone disease, or MBD.

For shelled creatures, the importance of maintaining good bone/shell strength is obvious. All you have to do is provide the foods that enable the chelonian to maintain this balance—and it's not complicated. Avoid feeding exclusively foods that are high in phosphorus and low in calcium. These include grapes, bananas, mealworms, crickets, and fresh peas.

With its oxalic acid content, spinach presents a special problem. This combines with calcium to form an insoluble salt, calcium oxalate, which builds up in the kidneys. Spinach should not be fed to chelonians. The ratio of calcium to phosphorus in the total diet, including supplements, should be a minimum of 2:1. Check the nutrition labels on the containers of packed turtle/tortoise foods and supplements for the proportions of calcium and phosphorous.

Aquatic turtles quickly learn to feed on commercial floating turtle food.

Vitamin D_3 and calcium: Vitamin D_3 assists the proper metabolism of calcium. Most calcium additives designed for reptile consumption now contain D_3. Improper metabolism of calcium or actual lack of calcium in the diet can result in soft bones and shell. Make certain that the diet you provide fulfills your chelonian's needs from the start. Should you acquire a turtle or tortoise with this deficiency, take the animal to your reptile veterinarian. Calcium injections can often stabilize or actually reverse the deterioration, and a better, more balanced diet will help prevent reoccurrence. Most turtles and tortoises will quickly develop bad dietary habits if the opportunity is presented. This includes those primarily herbivorous species that are fed more than minimal amounts of animal protein. A high protein diet will often cause improper shell growth as well.

Diet for Aquatic or Semiaquatic Turtles

Although most turtles in these categories consume some aquatic vegetation, most are quite carnivorous, eating aquatic insects, worms, crayfish, and snails. However, the sliders and cooters of the genera *Pseudemys* and *Trachemys* are more herbivorous, grazing extensively on aquatic plants such as Anacharis, Elodea, Hydrilla, and the various eelgrasses or turtle grasses. Captives will eat romaine, dandelion leaves and flowers, grated squash, aquarium plants, and other suitable dark, leafy vegetables (see caution regarding spinach, above), as well as grated fruits and some animal protein. Trout, catfish, and cat chows are excellent, and if used in moderation, many of the prepared turtle foods now on the market are satisfactory.

Diet for Terrestrial or Semiterrestrial Turtles

Contrary to popular belief, box turtles, like other terrestrial and semiterrestrial species, are not exclusively herbivorous or frugivorous. Although they will eat some fruit, the various box turtles eat worms, slugs, snails, insects, and carrion as well. The western box turtles (*Terrapene ornata* ssp.) are preferentially insectivorous. Newly born (pinky) mice will be eagerly accepted by most; many specimens will accept rehydrated trout, catfish, and cat chows. Many of the prepared turtle foods now on the market are excellent supplements.

Diet for Map Turtles

Insects and gastropod mollusks figure prominently in the diet of map turtles in the wild. Insects, worms, and snails are important to captive specimens as well. These turtles eat little vegetation but may pick at romaine and dandelion leaves as well as at aquarium plants. Trout, catfish, and cat chows, used in combination, seemingly form a good base diet for these active turtles.

Diet for Forest and Wooded Savanna Tortoises

Tortoise species such as red-footed, yellow-footed, and hinge-backs require a small to moderate amount of animal protein in their diet. Besides fruits and vegetables, some trout and catfish chow and low-fat cat chows should be provided. Star tortoises, elongated tortoises, and others of similar habits and habitats seem to do best when only small amounts of animal protein are provided.

Diet for Arid-Land Tortoises

The various European tortoises, leopard tortoises, both spur-thighed tortoises, radiated tortoises, and gopher and desert tortoises are predominantly herbivorous. They should be given well-rounded vegetable diets and very little fruit. Among other things we provide romaine, escarole, bok choy, okra, a few green beans, bean sprouts, alfalfa sprouts, rabbit pellets, dandelion leaves and flowers, and grated squash. We provide a very little rehydrated, low-fat cat chow about once a month.

How Often Should Food Be Offered?

The intake of food by turtles and tortoises will vary according to their metabolic rate. Being ectotherms, with the body temperature close to that of the environment, the bodily functions of chelonians are more active when they are warm than when they are cold. When a turtle or tortoise becomes too cold, digestion can stop and putrefaction can occur in the gut, causing distress or even death.

Optimum temperatures for most turtles and tortoises are between 78 and 90°F (25.5–32.2°C). (For more specific information, see species accounts beginning on page 46.) Even on cooler days, if the sun is shining, the chelonians will bask (thermoregulate) and raise their body temperatures well above the ambient. Aquatic species accomplish this by either hauling out on the bank, clambering up on an exposed snag or rock, or floating at the surface of the water. When it is cool and conditions do not permit thermoregulation, turtles become lethargic and inactive.

When they are at their optimum warmth, turtles and tortoises will eat surprisingly large amounts of food daily. When they are cooler, less food is necessary. When they are cooler yet, such as when you are preparing them for hibernation, food should be withheld entirely (see chapter on hibernating, page 43).

Deprived in captivity of space for normal activity, turtles and tortoises can become unhealthily obese. Many advanced hobbyists use scales to watch the weight of their specimens. Far less sophisticated, our method is to know the specimen. It is not difficult to see signs of weight loss or gain and to alter the dietary offerings accordingly.

What If the Diet Has Been Wrong?

As mentioned earlier, chelonians can become very fond of, even addicted to, incorrect diets. This is unhealthy and must be altered at the earliest opportunity. If you continue to offer them the dietary items to which they are accustomed, as well as provide the correct new foods, your pets will often resist the change. In most cases, the quickest and best way to effect the change is to withhold the incorrect foods while providing ample amounts of the correct ones. Your turtle or tortoise may rebel by not eating for a day, a week, even a fortnight (or longer), but when sufficiently hungry it *will* eat. For the most reluctant specimens, you may wish to smear small amounts of their favored foods on the new kinds. Sometimes just adding the scent of the previous food will facilitate the acceptance of the better food by your shelled pet.

Although this may seem cruel to you, in the long run it is much kinder than subjecting your turtle or tortoise to diet-related maladies such as metabolic bone disease or visceral gout. If you suspect that diet-related health problems are already present, consult your veterinarian.

Shortcuts to Proper Feeding

In this case, the term "shortcut" relates mostly to proper storage and the purchase of prepackaged diets. Prepacked vegetable salad mixtures are available in many stores. You may find purchasing these more suitable than mixing your own tortoise food. There is nothing wrong with this, but we suggest that if spinach is a part of the purchased mixture that all (or at least most) of it be removed. Do not use badly wilted or discolored vegetables.

Prepacked turtle and tortoise foods, many of them claiming to be "complete diets," are also now available. While some of these may be suitable for a "base diet," we suggest that all be augmented with fresh natural items.

Rather than search for worms every time we need them, we collect all that we can when they are abundant (such as after dark on sidewalks and roads, following a spring or autumn rain) and we set up a worm-holding facility in a cool area. That sure beats hefting a shovel every time a turtle acts hungry.

We also buy crickets and mealworms wholesale. You can often work out a cheaper price with your local pet store or you may choose to buy from a wholesaler. Either way, it will save you money. Wholesalers advertise in the various reptile and amphibian magazines listed in the Useful Addresses and Literature section (page 112).

Turtle and Tortoise Defenses

The shell of a turtle or tortoise is not its only defense. Chelonians of many species have developed other ploys, from camouflage to biting, as additional safeguards.

Camouflage: Just try to make out the outline of a big leopard tortoise resting in the dappled shade beneath a shrub or that of an Indian star tortoise in the tangled grasses of a dry savanna. Or try to find the domed, algae-covered carapace of a mud turtle in the water-smoothed, algae-covered stones of a pond bottom; the carapace of a snapping turtle in the submerged snags and detritus of its pond-bottom home; or the vague outline of a soft-shelled turtle, buried under sand. Camouflage works!

Shells: The shells of many turtles and tortoises are modified to provide varying degrees of protection. The plastron (bottom shell) of New World mud turtles has two hinges that allow it to be drawn upward. Since, even when thus closed, the small plastron does not entirely cover the soft parts, the value of the hinges seems questionable. In contrast, the large, single-hinged plastron of the American and Asiatic box turtles provides nearly complete protection. African mud turtles also have a fairly large, single-hinged plastron that provides considerable (but not complete) protection when closed.

Few tortoises have hinged plastra. Of these few, the plastral hinge of the seldom seen little spider tortoise of Madagascar is best developed.

Despite its large size and rather gaudy coloration, this leopard tortoise, Geochelone pardalis babcocki, *virtually disappears in the filigree shadows of a small bush . . .*

. . . but is conspicuous in the open.

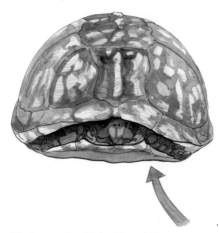

The box turtle with its hinged plastron presents an almost impenetrable defense.

Of all turtles and tortoises, only the members of the African tortoise genus *Kinixys*, all aptly called hinge-backed tortoises, have a carapacial (top shell) hinge. When drawn against the plastron, the steeply domed posterior carapace helps protect the rear limbs and tail.

When startled or threatened, some turtles and tortoises withdraw their heads into their shells and fold their

The retiring tortoise prefers to hide when threatened.

usually heavily scaled forelimbs across the anterior shell opening. This is especially well noted among the more terrestrial (wood and leaf turtles) species.

Other defenses: There are some turtles that are simply unable to withdraw their heads. Among these, the skull is often massive and the mandibles formidably strong (big-headed and snapping turtles). In some cases, the neck is also elongated (common snapping turtle), providing a great reach when a defensive bite is attempted.

Many of the more secretive aquatic and semiaquatic species have additional defenses. The odor from scent glands gives the musk turtles their common names of "stinking-Jims" or "stinkpots." If lifted or carelessly handled, many turtles, especially the snappers and soft-shells, kick and scratch with long legs and sharp claws.

Some turtles that seem rather poorly adapted for protection through striking and biting, indulge in defensive posturing (fully extended hind legs), thus tilting their shell toward the aggressor and lunging forward. This "butting" motion apparently acts as a predator deterrent.

The largely unprotected heads and necks of the sideneck turtles seem curiously vulnerable. Although in many cases the extra length of the carapace and the plastron offers protection from above and below, from the front the neck and head are virtually unprotected. Perhaps camouflage, cryptic coloration and markings, and the exudate from the scent glands deter most predators.

The various aquatic soft-shelled turtles of the family Trionychidae also have long necks and formidable jaw power.

Hiding: Baby tortoises and turtles of both aquatic and terrestrial species are more secretive than the adults. Tortoise babies often remain in grassy or brushy cover, box and wood turtles amidst leaf litter and woodland detritus, and aquatic species near or amidst submerged vegetation and thick snags. Babies of sedentary aquatic species (snappers and soft-shells) hide in submerged fallen leaves or bury themselves in the muddy/sandy substrate of their ponds and rivers.

Eyesight: Turtles and tortoises have very acute eyesight and the merest movement of a distant (potential) predator will send basking aquatics into the water or cause strolling terrestrials to become quiescent. No matter what size or age they may be, turtles instinctively know that being overlooked by predators is, quite simply, the best defense of all.

A Silent Predator

Although the findings are not yet conclusive, it is likely that the various fire ants are among the most serious predators of turtles and tortoises. This is especially so in the United States, where, since introduced fire ants have no natural enemies, they are now more numerous acre by acre than even in their native tropical American strongholds.

The problem is this: the natural reaction of most turtles and tortoises to pain is to withdraw into their shells and remain stationary until the offending object has left. If this reaction is in response to a fire ant attack, the turtle can soon be overcome and killed by the insects.

But the ants attack more than the adult chelonians. Fire ants are especially effective at locating hatching eggs and overcoming the emerging baby chelonians. The various American box turtles are among the species most seriously threatened by the ever-increasing fire ant scourge. Although total eradication of fire ants is now unlikely, stringent control of fire ant populations in wild areas is of paramount importance to both wildlife and humans.

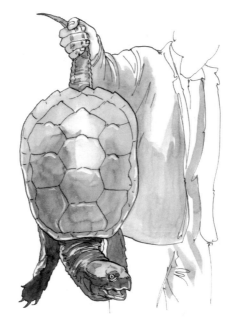

Large snapping turtles can only be handled safely this way.

Soft-shelled turtles like to bury themselves in the sand or loose gravel in their tank, leaving only their nose-tip exposed.

Health and Medications

Whether the initial cost of a turtle or tortoise be small or great, we feel that your pet deserves the very best care that can be provided. When it becomes ill, this includes veterinary observation. Your turtle or tortoise did not ask to be taken from the wild; the owning of one is a responsibility that should not be taken lightly.

By providing your turtle or tortoise with a suitable regimen—cleanliness, healthy diet, and a warm, stress-free environment—you can minimize the potential for health problems, but you can never eradicate the possibility of sickness.

As you would with any other pet, find a veterinarian who is qualified to offer care and treatment to your chelonian. Reptilian veterinary medicine is a specialized field. Not all veterinarians choose, or are qualified, to provide treatment to turtles or tortoises. You should find someone qualified before the need arises. That said, let's look at a few of the problems that you may encounter.

"Simple" fungal infections: Aquatic turtles may develop fuzzy gray and white patches that are actually fungal growths. Soft-shelled turtles are especially prone to this problem, and poor water quality is a major cause. Acriflavin, readily available in aquarium and pet stores, will often eradicate fungal infections when added to the water. If the growths persist, consult a veterinarian.

Swollen eyelids and peeling skin: Acute Vitamin A deficiency causes swollen eyelids, which result in vision problems as well as flaking, peeling, and often bloody skin patches.

Although acute Vitamin A deficiency is not often encountered, it occurs most commonly in rapidly growing hatchling and juvenile specimens that have had their usually incorrect diets supplemented with only D_3/calcium additives. Injectable Vitamin A may reverse the problem and a better, more balanced diet and multivitamins (rather than just D_3) will prevent its reoccurrence.

Several things other than Vitamin A deficiency can cause swollen eyelids and impaired vision in turtles and tortoises. Among other causes are insufficient humidity, old age, advanced systemic disease, and improper diet. A treatment of topical and/or systemic antibiotics is mandatory. Consult your veterinarian.

Obesity: This is as dangerous to turtles and tortoises as to any other animals. In cases of gross obesity, the functions of the liver and other organs are impaired. Correcting the diet in both quality and quantity is recommended.

Respiratory disease: Clogged or runny nostrils, gasping with open mouth and wheezing, inability to submerge (aquatic species), excessive mucus in the nose and mouth, and bubbling or foaming at the nose and/or mouth indicate serious respiratory problems. The causes can be numerous, singly or in combination. Respiratory disease can be lingering or rapidly fatal. Antibiotic treatment is mandatory but may differ according to the causative agent. Make your pet comfortable by making sure that the cage is warm enough, or that the patient is utilizing the hot-spot, and consult your veterinarian immediately!

Ear infections: Ear infections, usually abscesses, resulting from overheating and a humidity too low for the species involved, are not uncommon in terrestrial chelonians, and are quite common in box turtles. We have seen abscesses more rarely on aquatic turtles; poor water quality is most usually the cause in these cases.

Reptilian abscesses do not respond positively to systemic treatments. The abscesses should be surgically removed by a veterinarian. Once the caseous material is removed, the site must be cleaned and bandaged daily. The flushing and dressing is often a simple matter that can be performed at home, but on strong chelonians that remain withdrawn for long periods, veterinary help may continue to be needed.

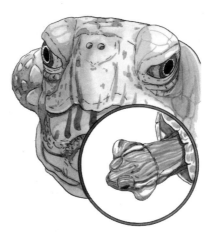

Face abscesses, on box turtles (top) and water turtles (inset), look like large lumps.

Mouth infections: Mouth infections may vary from abscesses to acute infectious stomatitis—literally an infection of the stoma (mouth); also called mouthrot. Abscesses should be surgically removed. Determining what antibiotic to use against the pathogen will require sensitivity tests. Stomatitis can be fatal; it can quickly progress from tissue to bone structure. If it progresses to the tissues surrounding the trachea the chelonian may suffocate. In all cases consult your veterinarian.

Shell-rot (ulcerative shell disease): Usually of bacterial origin, certain fungi may also be implicated in shell-rot. Injuries, including burns, bruises, and abrasions that cause breaks in the shell surface, coupled with unsatisfactory hygiene, provide footholds for this disease. Most bacteria implicated are gram-negative varieties. The causative agents must be defined and treated with appropriate antiseptics or antibiotics. While combating this problem, complete sterilization of the quarters, from substrate to heaters, must be done daily. In severely active cases, surgical removal of infected shell areas

may be necessary. Untreated cases can be fatal. Consult your veterinarian immediately.

Shell breaks/injuries: Depending on the severity, taping (minor injuries), flushing with antibiotic treatment, and debridement of fragmented shell pieces will be necessary. Fiberglass reconstruction may also be an option. Consult your veterinarian immediately.

Ectoparasites (ticks, leeches, and bot fly larvae): Terrestrial chelonians collected from the wild may have from one to many ticks attached. These may be removed, after they have been relaxed with a drop of rubbing alcohol or mineral oil, by grasping them and pulling gently, but firmly. Be certain the embedded mouth parts are removed. Leeches may be found on newly collected aquatic turtles or terrestrial tropical species. A dab of salt on the leech will cause it to loosen its grip and it can then be removed with forceps or fingers. Certain parasitic flies may lay their eggs on the soft areas of a chelonian's skin. The larvae hatch and burrow beneath the skin. These should be surgically removed by a veterinarian as

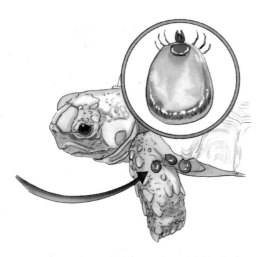

Inspect your tortoise or terrestrial turtle for external parasites such as ticks.

quickly as they are noticed. Bathe the incised area with antiseptics.

Endoparasites: Over the course of their lives, many chelonians—even those that are captive-bred and hatched—may be found to have internal parasites. An occasional fecal float and/or mucus swab can determine whether parasites are present. If present, to be effectively purged, these parasites must be properly identified. Because of the complexities of identification of endoparasites, the necessity to accurately weigh specimens to be treated, and the need to measure

Medical abbreviations

mg —milligram
  (1 mg = 0.001 gram)
kg —kilogram
  (1000 grams; 2.2 pounds)
mcg —microgram
  (1 mcg = 0.000001 gram)
IM —intramuscularly
IP —intraperitoneally
PO —orally

purge dosages, the eradication of internal parasites is best left to a qualified reptile veterinarian. Following are a few of the recommended medications and dosages, which are usually based on the weight of the animal. These medications and dosages were suggested by Dr. Richard Funk, a specialist reptile veterinarian of Tampa, Florida.

Amoebas and Trichomonads

40–50 mg/kg of **Metronidazole** orally. The treatment is repeated in two weeks.

Dimetridazole can also be used but the dosage is very different. 40–50 mg/kg of Dimetridazole is administered daily for five days. The treatment is then repeated in two weeks. All treatments with both medications are administered once daily.

Coccidia

Many treatments are available.

The dosages of **sulfadiazine, sulfamerazine,** and **sulfamethazine** are identical. Administer 75 mg/kg the first day, then follow up for the next five days with 45 mg/kg. All treatments orally and once daily.

Sulfadimethoxine is also effective. The initial dosage is 90 mg/kg orally to be followed on the next five days with 45 mg/kg orally. All dosages are administered once daily.

Trimethoprim-sulfa may also be used. 30 mg/kg should be administered once daily for seven days.

Cestodes (=Tapeworms)

Several effective treatments are available.

Bunamidine may be administered orally at a dosage of 50 mg/kg. A second treatment occurs in two weeks.

Niclosamide, orally, at a dosage of 150 mg/kg, is also effective. A second treatment is given in two weeks.

Praziquantel may be administered either orally or intramuscularly. The dosage is 5–8 mg/kg and is to be repeated in two weeks.

Trematodes (Flukes)

Praziquantel at 8 mg/kg may be administered either orally or intramuscularly. The treatment is repeated in two weeks. Some veterinarians prefer the oral administration.

Nematodes (Roundworms)

Several effective treatments are available.

Levamisole, an injectable intraperitoneal treatment, should be administered at a dosage of 10 mg/kg and the treatment repeated in two weeks.

Ivermectin, injected intramuscularly in a dosage of 200 mcg/kg is effective. The treatment is to be repeated in two weeks. Some veterinarians prefer oral administration of this medication. Ivermectin can be toxic to certain taxa.

Thiabendazole and **Fenbendazole** have similar dosages. Both are administered orally at 50–100 mg/kg and repeated in two weeks.

Mebendazole is administered orally at a dosage of 20–25 mg/kg and repeated in two weeks.

Oral Worming: A New Technique

Andy Highfield, Director of the Tortoise Trust of the United Kingdom, has shared the following method of worming difficult-to-handle turtles and tortoises that feed on land.

One of the more regularly used methods of purging tortoises of endoparasites involves the use of a stomach tube, a method difficult with large and/or strong specimens.

Highfield suggests an alternative: apply to favorite food items a paste of Fenbendazole often used for livestock

Some medications, such as paste vermifuges, can be placed on food before being fed to solitary chelonians.

(Panacur Paste for Horses). The tortoises eagerly consume the paste-smeared feed. The recommended dosage is 100 mg/kg each day for five days. Two weeks later the treatment is repeated for three days.

Panacur Paste for Horses contains 3.5mg of Fenbendazole in each 20g of paste. This equates to about 19 percent and may be considered a concentration of 20 percent for all practical purposes.

Panacur is tolerated well by turtles and tortoises and is considered the purge of preference. This method of worming has proven stress-free and effective at Highfield's facility.

Other maladies—from arthritic problems and broken bones to complex infections—are known to afflict chelonians. Veterinary consultation, assessment, and treatment are necessary for most of these problems.

Breeding

While casual hobbyists may be content merely to keep a turtle or two healthy over the years, many enthusiasts progress well beyond that stage. As a matter of fact, as the wild populations diminish, if we hope to continue to have many of our shelled friends available to us as pets for many more years, we must do all possible to keep captive populations stable or increasing through captive breeding efforts.

Over the years, cheloniophiles have learned how to breed many kinds of turtles and tortoises. Suggestions for various species are in the individual species accounts. But here we would like to familiarize you with some of the generalities.

Basics

All turtles and tortoises reproduce by means of eggs, which like the eggs of birds, *must* be laid on land. But not all eggs are fertile; mature females can and often do lay clutches of perfectly formed but infertile eggs. Females are also capable of "sperm storage," laying several clutches of fertile eggs after a single mating.

Following copulation, the first clutch of eggs may be laid in three to six weeks. Many species of turtles and tortoises "multi-clutch" annually—that is they lay more than a single clutch of eggs each year. How long it takes for the eggs to hatch is dictated by species and by nest temperature and humidity. Excessive heat, cold, moisture, or dryness can kill or deform the embryo. The eggs of many species of turtles and tortoises undergo a diapause—a cessation of embryonic development—for a varying period of time. The diapause may last from only a few days to several weeks. The diapause is often triggered by incubation conditions (such as moisture and temperature) that differ in some way from optimum, but which are actually necessary to embryonic development. In the wild, this may help ensure that the young are hatched at an optimal time for survival.

Reproductive Cycling

The breeding sequences of turtles and tortoises in the wild are triggered largely by external stimuli. Photoperiods, seasonal weather changes (whether these are the traditional annual progression of the seasons of the temperate world or merely the change from dry to rainy season in the tropical areas), hibernation (when applicable), changing barometric pressure, and temperature all contribute significantly to the breeding readiness of most species. Indispensable with all of these, of course, is the coming together of the two sexes at the proper times.

The reproductive sequences of temperate turtle and tortoises species are controlled by all five of the above factors. Those of tropical species are controlled by the dry-to-rainy seasonal changes, fluctuations in barometric pressure (low pressures, such as those accompanying the passage of a frontal system or a typhoon often induce breeding behavior), and the encountering of a sexually receptive mate.

It may be necessary to reproduce some or all of these conditions to induce breeding. Even then, our efforts may fail.

Breeding Parameters

	PP	SST	SSR	BP	H
Parameters needed to prepare temperate species for breeding	5	4	3	2	3*
Parameters needed to prepare tropical species for breeding	2	2	4	4	0

PP = natural photoperiod; SST = seasonal temperature fluctuations; SSR = seasonal rain/humidity increase; BP = barometric pressure fluctuation; H = hibernation. The numbers used indicate increasing importance on a scale of 1 to 5. 0 = not applicable.
* = see comment on hibernation.

Hibernation: The importance of hibernation to chelonians physiologically adapted to hibernate is largely unknown. (See the chapter "Seasonal Behavior and Hibernation," page 43). Certainly temperate turtles can be kept, and even bred for a few years, without being hibernated. This has been amply proven by breeding successes with wood turtles and Hermann's tortoises kept in outside facilities in southern Florida. However, many breeders have reported a decline in the viability of eggs laid after a few years of nonhibernation by their wood turtles. Since there are no properly hibernated control specimens available for comparison, it is unknown whether the nonhibernation or some other factor is at fault.

Finding a mate: How do solitary turtles and tortoises find a receptive mate? In their favor is the fact that chelonians are creatures of habit and have a tremendously well-developed homing instinct. They can wander far on land or in water and unerringly return to the tiny area where they hatched. In many cases these treks, or at least the destination of the trek, will bring a given chelonian into contact with others of its own kind. Turtles and tortoises also have remarkable visual acuity. They can probably see other turtles as readily as they see predators. Many chelonians produce pheromones, scented hormones relating to reproduction. Since the producing glands enlarge during periods of reproductive activity, it is surmised that the pheromone output is greater, and may be scented somewhat differently. Certainly terrestrial species can trail each other for long distances by homing in on the pheromones. The role of pheromone dispersal is less well understood with aquatic species.

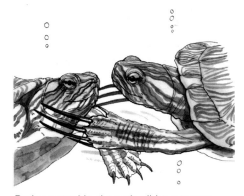

During courtship, the male slider or cooter will use his long front claws to stroke the face of the female.

Courtship and copulation: Aquatic and semiaquatic turtles breed while in the water. Some of the courtships, also performed in the water, are intricate and prolonged. Sexually mature males of many species of slider and painted turtles develop greatly lengthened foreclaws that are vibrated and used for stroking the face, neck, and forelimbs of receptive females, while the pair is hovering in mid-water. Other species of aquatic or semiaquatic turtles indulge in stylized vertical head nods or lateral waves of the head and neck while the pair is submerged.

Some species of terrestrial and semiterrestrial *turtles* may indulge in courtship and breed while on land. Other species may begin courtship on land but breed in the water. A few species, terrestrial throughout most of the year, may seek the water for hibernation and accomplish courtship and breeding just before or after hibernation.

Tortoises court and breed while on land. The courtship of many terrestrial turtles and tortoises is harsh, involving rendering the female immobile by biting or nipping at her head, neck, limbs, and anterior carapace and/or ramming her carapace with that of the male whose head is withdrawn during the procedure. Copulation may be accompanied by shell bumping, biting at the back of the female's head or neck if she extends either, or by head nods and gruff vocalizations (squeals, chuckles, or grunts) by the male.

Nesting area: No matter whether the species is aquatic, semiaquatic, or terrestrial, you must provide a suitable earthen nesting area. Chelonians that are well-acclimated will most often nest as naturally as they would in the wild. In rare cases the female may simply lay her small clutch atop a protected grass hummock or under loose leaf litter. However, most females actually dig a well-defined nest, to whatever depth they are able to reach with their hind legs. The nesting soil must be deep enough to accommodate the efforts of the female. The soil should be barely dampened so it holds its shape as it is being dug. Collapsing sides or insufficient depth of nesting medium may force the female to discontinue her nesting attempt. The females of a very few species may initially shove dirt or debris aside with the front of the plastron, creating a broad, shallow depression. After completing this to their satisfaction, they will then pivot and dig with their rear legs. According to the species, the nest may be tapered, flasked, or straight-sided.

As she digs, the female turtle or tortoise may moisten the soil with water from her bladder. As the eggs are laid, the female reaches down into the pit with a hind foot and positions each egg. The descent of the dropping eggs may be slowed somewhat by the expulsion of a thick, viscous fluid from the female's vent. Once the clutch is completed, the female covers the nest

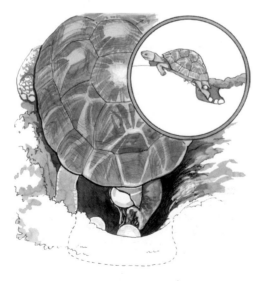

The female radiated tortoise digs a vertical burrow for egg deposition.

with the loosened soil and methodically tamps down the covering.

Removal of eggs: If we are present, we often remove the eggs as they are being laid. To do this we merely scoop out the back side of the hole so that we may maneuver without bumping the female. If we are not present, we carefully dig up the eggs at our earliest convenience, and place them in small plastic containers half-filled with dampened vermiculite; the containers are then put into the incubator.

Note: After incubation has begun, it is important that the eggs *not* be rotated on either longitudinal axis. To help us with egg orientation, we pencil a small "X" on the top of each egg before it is moved. Reptile eggs, unlike bird eggs, do not require turning during incubation (nor once incubating can reptile eggs survive turning through the end of the second trimester). They are able to survive some turning during the final trimester, but there is no reason to do so.

Our tip: If your turtle or tortoise enclosure is outside, keep an eye on the female as she prepares the nesting site. Crows, magpies, and bluejays watch a nesting female and summon others of their kind. They steal and eat the eggs as they are laid. If you are in an area with fire ants, do not let the eggs hatch in the ground. The ants will find and eat the hatching young.

Incubation: Chelonian eggs require warmth—77 to 86°F (25–30°C)— and moisture to develop. During the summer, the eggs of temperate species of turtle/tortoises will usually develop satisfactorily at high normal room temperature—77 to 80°F (25–26.6°C). Tropical species, or species from warmer microhabitats in temperate areas of either the southern or northern hemisphere (deserts, etc.), will need to be kept a little warmer than normal room temperatures—80 to 86°F (26.6–30°C). We keep our incubators set at 84 to 86°F (28.8–30°C), a range satisfactory for most tropical species, but the eggs of red-footed and yellow-footed tortoises would develop more reliably at between 78 and 82°F (25.5–27.7°C).

It seems as if each hobbyist has a preferred way of incubating the eggs. Among other mediums, substrates of torn newspaper, perlite, soil, sand, and vermiculite have been suggested. We prefer vermiculite. The amount of water we mix with the vermiculite varies by species. The eggs of rain forest tortoises and aquatic turtles, for example, require a greater amount of moisture than the eggs of arid-land or desert species. To moisten the vermiculite, add water and mix until the vermiculite clumps together when squeezed in your hand. The volumes will be about four parts vermiculite to one part water, but add that water sparingly; you may need less. When the mixture clumps when squeezed, that's the consistency to use for forestland species. For desert species, squeeze the vermiculite until you squeeze out a little of the water, or use less water to start with. One third to one half of the height of the egg should be nestled into the vermiculite.

If we choose to retain a high relative humidity for some of the eggs, the dampened vermiculite and eggs are placed in small covered containers inside the incubator. It is usually best to leave the top off the small containers that hold the eggs of arid-land species. In both cases, we place an open Styrofoam cup of water in the bottom of the incubator. If it becomes necessary to remoisten the substrate, take care *not* to wet the eggs.

Starting the hatchlings: Assisted by some biodegrading of the shell, the hatchlings cut their way free of the egg with an "egg tooth" or caruncle (this tooth drops off in a few days). It may take a day or longer for the hatchling to

Hatchling chelonians use an egg tooth to open their egg.

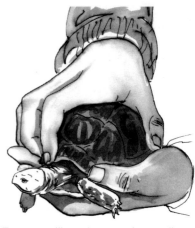

Even a small tortoise or turtle can slip out of your grasp, so use two hands.

finally emerge from the egg. When they emerge from their eggs, hatchling chelonians usually have large umbilical egg sacs. These are absorbed in several hours to about two days. The hatchlings will not need, or even want, to feed until the egg sac has been fully utilized.

Hatchling chelonians, like the young of any living creature, are delicate.

Take care that the babies are not on a substrate sufficiently abrasive to rupture the yolk sac. We often keep our hatchlings on dampened paper towels inside their own terrarium until the yolk sac has been absorbed.

We assure all hatchlings with even warmth for the first few weeks of their life. Once the sac is gone, we provide them with large amounts of suitable

Here we see two stages in the hatching of a radiated tortoise, Geochelone radiata.

Even a large yolk sac such as seen on this hatchling radiated tortoise will be absorbed within 48 hours.

food. Hatchling tortoises are provided with daily drinking water; hatchling aquatic and semiaquatics are provided with clean water of sufficient depth to enable them to swim. Haul-out areas are nonabrasive and very accessible. Floating plants or other such cover are provided. The hatchlings of some semiterrestrials (such as wood and bog turtles) often do best if kept for the first few weeks in a small flat container containing about one-quarter inch (.6 cm) of warm water and provided with a hiding area. The hiding area can be an artificial "cave"; if unmilled sphagnum moss is provided, the turtles make their own hiding area.

Protect hatchlings from predators and overheating if they are taken outside. Remember that jays, crows, and grackles are as avid predators as raccoons, and unfiltered sunlight can overheat a small container to a lethal temperature in a very short time.

HOW-TO:
Make Your Own Incubator

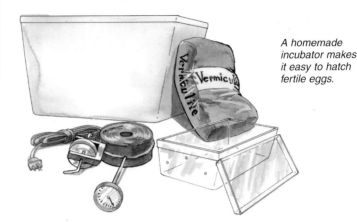

A homemade incubator makes it easy to hatch fertile eggs.

Materials needed for one incubator:

1 wafer thermostat/heater (obtainable from feed stores; these are commonly used in incubators for chicks)

1 thermometer

1 heat tape

1 Styrofoam cooler—with thick sides (a fish shipping box is ideal)

Using a paring knife to make the holes in the lid for the thermostat and thermometer.

Place the heat tape in a series of loops on the bottom of the cooler. Attach the leads of the heat tape to the appropriate leads of the thermostat.

Poke a hole through the lid of the cooler, and suspend the thermostat/heater from the inside. Add another hole for a thermometer, so you can check on the inside temperature without opening the top. If there's

no flange on the thermometer to keep it from slipping through the hole in the lid, use a rubber band wound several times around the thermometer to form a flange.

Put the lid on the cooler, and plug in the thermostat/heater. Wait half an hour and check the temperature. Adjust the thermostat/heater until the temperature inside the incubator is about 80 to 86°F (26.6–30°C). (See the species accounts so you'll know what temperature to use.) The

L-pin "handle" on the top of the thermostat is the rheostat.

Once you have the temperature regulated, put the container of eggs inside the incubator and close the lid.

Check the temperature daily, use the rheostat to increase or decrease the temperature, and add a little water to the incubating medium as needed. Keep the humidity high for aquatic/semi-terrestrial species and fairly low for tortoise species from xeric areas.

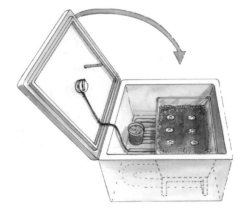

Once the heat tape is wired to the thermostat and the unit plugged in, you can add the container of eggs.

Seasonal Behavior and Hibernation

The behavior of turtles and tortoises is affected by external stimuli. Because turtles are poikilothermic (cold-blooded), ambient temperature plays a big part in their overall activity patterns. But seasonal factors such as photoperiod and barometric pressure also influence chelonian activities.

Seasonal "slowing": Although tropical species of chelonians may become dormant for short periods of time (triggered by excessive drought or heat), these species are not physiologically programmed to hibernate or estivate (brumate). On the other hand, even where temperatures do not become prohibitively cold, temperate turtle and tortoise species slow their activities and may actually hibernate for 30, 60, or even 90 days. In this case, it would seem that the cessation of activity is caused more (or at least as much) by waning day lengths than by lowered ambient temperatures.

Whether tropical or temperate in origin, captive chelonians can be induced to remain active year-round by creating artificially long day lengths with electric bulbs and by keeping the animals warm. That the turtles know something is amiss is often attested by diminished appetites and inordinate lethargy during the months they would normally be resting.

Is denial of hibernation healthy for them? We simply don't know—at least we don't know over the long run. We do know that after a few years a chelonian denied hibernation seems to produce larger numbers of inviable eggs. We have also found that, even with suitable warmth, many temperate turtles seem to be more susceptible to respiratory ailments when kept active during the months of winter.

We prefer to hibernate our own chelonians that would normally do so in the wild and that are healthy enough to withstand the procedure.

Hibernation is not necessarily stress-free for chelonians, whether in the wild or in captivity. Death is far from a stranger at these times. If your turtle or tortoise is not in A-1 condition, do not hibernate it. And you *must* know where your specimen originated. It may be that not all populations of a given species hibernate; for instance, spotted turtles from Massachusetts certainly hibernate each winter. Spotted turtles from Florida don't need to hibernate, although they may enter into brief wintertime periods of dormancy.

For semiterrestrial turtles or tortoises, hibernation can be accomplished in two ways—"natural" (on their own) and "artificial" (with a little help from you), but we will recommend only the artificial way for aquatic species. Because of the probability of fluctuating temperatures, the natural way is more of a gamble for tortoises as well. If you do intend to hibernate your specimens, they must be heavy (but not overtly fat), be parasite free, have no signs of respiratory distress, and be free of any other signs of illness or disease.

HOW-TO:
Hibernate Your Turtle

Hibernation basics: When you hibernate your chelonian, you place it within a hibernation chamber or hibernaculum and place the hibernaculum in a cool area for several weeks. The ideal hibernation temperature—the range you will be striving for—is from 38 to 45°F (3.3–7.2°C). The humidity of the hibernaculum will vary by species, being higher for aquatic and semi-aquatic species than for arid-land forms. The hibernation period may vary from as few as 60 to as many as 120 days.

Before hibernation: One of the most critical factors is actually a prehibernation concern. A turtle's or tortoise's gut *must* be empty of food before the animal is hibernated. A chelonian's rate of digestion varies with ambient temperature. Warm days and warm nights promote rapid digestion. Warm days and

Give your turtle or tortoise a hearty meal 2 to 4 weeks before you place the animal in hibernation.

Placing your chelonian in a shallow dish of warm water will encourage defecation before the animal is hibernated.

cool nights favor slower digestion, and cool days and cool nights make for *very* slow digestion. Thus, you must know your animal and stop feeding it from two weeks (warm areas) to four weeks (cool areas) before it is allowed to hibernate. An occasional soak in warm water may hasten defecation. Err on the side of safety. Continue to provide water throughout the prehibernation fast.

Natural hibernation: If you live in a temperate area and keep your turtles or tortoises outdoors, Eastern, three-toed, ornate, and desert box turtles and Hermann's and Central Asian tortoises are the most likely candidates for natural hibernation. These chelonians all naturally hibernate on land and are quite adept at finding suitable niches even in captivity. You must ascertain that they dig well below the frost line. Many hobbyists in the northern United States add a cover of 1 foot (30 cm) or so of fallen leaves after the chelonians have dug in and have entered dormancy. Do make certain that the turtles/tor-

toises have not dug into a flood-prone area. Remember also that predators, from domestic dogs to raccoons and bears, will willingly dine on hibernating turtle if the opportunity presents itself. Use necessary precautions. Make sure the area is fenced, or that the hibernaculum is covered with wire netting. You must also watch that the chelonians do not

Fire ants, now commonplace throughout the Gulf states and westward to California, prey on ground nesting animals such as turtles and tortoises.

Shrews, with their digging skills, acute smelling ability, and prodigious appetites, can make quick work of a hibernating turtle or tortoise.

emerge from hibernation during any unnaturally warm periods. If they emerge, they should be brought indoors to finish their hibernation cycle or be warmed and fed from that point onward. If at any time you are able to tell that a chelonian has urinated during its dormancy, it is best to rouse the specimen and let it drink before either continuing hibernation or warming it for the remainder of the season.

Artificial hibernation may be arranged in several ways. Because we live in a mild climate, we have found that the best method for us involves using a modified refrigerator.

Each aquatic and semiterrestrial turtle is placed in an individual plastic box that is filled with moist, unmilled sphagnum moss. The turtles, boxes and all, are then placed in a refrigerator modified to retain temperatures at between 40 and 44°F (4.4–6.6°C). The turtles are checked periodically and are roused for the duration should we feel all is not well. Light weight and sunken eyes or respirations are types of such indicators.

The hibernating tortoises are housed in the same cooling

Nestle the chelonian in container of damp sphagnum moss . . .

and place that container in a larger insulated box.

unit, but are in deeper plastic boxes filled with dried leaves or dry sphagnum. The condition of each tortoise is checked at two-week intervals. Again, should we feel a problem exists (it seldom does) the tortoise is roused, warmed, and kept active for the duration.

In cooler areas, turtles and tortoises are often hibernated in root cellars or other such underground "steady temperature" storage areas that retain cool temperatures of 35 to 45°F (1.6–7.2°C). In these areas tortoises are hibernated using two boxes, one inside the other with insulating material between (Styrofoam peanuts are ideal). The inner box contains the tortoise and leaves or other basically inert material that is not prone to mildew or mold. Neither straw nor hay is recommended for use either in the inner box or between the two boxes. Keep an eye on temperatures. Even with heavy insulation, sustained temperatures below freezing will prove devastating or fatal to the turtle or tortoise. The temperature inside the hibernaculum should be from 40 to 44°F (4.4–6.6°C).

At the end of the hibernation period, when ground temperatures naturally warm, those turtles or tortoises that are hibernating naturally will simply wake up and dig themselves out. For those that you are hibernating, simply bring the hibernaculum to normal room temperature and allow the chelonians to awaken.

Alligator Snappers and Common Snappers

The Alligator Snapper

The alligator snapping turtle, *Macroclemys temminckii*, and its single close relative, the common snapping turtle, *Chelydra serpentina*, are the only living members of the family Chelydridae.

The alligator snapping turtle is a monotypic species (a single species as described—no subspecies) found in larger river systems and lakes and oxbows of the southeastern coastal plain and the Mississippi River drainages. It is not only the largest species of freshwater turtle found in the United States; it is also one of the largest (and may, in fact, be the heaviest) in the world. Adult males weighing over 150 pounds (68 kg)—the record for a wild specimen is 251 pounds (114 kg); for a long-term captive, 316 pounds (143 kg)—are well documented. Straight measure carapace lengths of more than 25 inches (63.5 cm)—record 31½ inches (80 cm); Conant/Collins 1991—are also known for males.

The females are the smaller of the two sexes, and there is speculation that it is the midsize males that are the most consistent breeders. It may be fact that the largest males are either too far past prime or simply too large to breed effectively with the considerably smaller females.

Appearance: Rather than attractive or prepossessing, the alligator snapper is exactly the opposite. It has a roughened, mud-brown carapace, a tiny plastron, a grossly oversized head, correspondingly powerful, hooked jaws, and a roughened tail that is nearly as long as the carapace. Dermal tubercles and projections are abundant on the sides of the head, chin, and neck. The forelimbs are heavily scaled.

The young of this species are even more roughened than the adults. The carapace is concave on its front margin, roughly parallel on the sides, and both convex and heavily serrate posteriorly. Once past the vulnerable juvenile stage, the alligator snapper needs little protection from any enemy (potential or actual) but humans.

Macroclemys are among the most persistently aquatic of turtles. It is speculated that females leave the water only for the purpose of egg-laying.

Breeding: As are all turtles, the alligator snapping turtle is oviparous. Depending upon temperatures and latitude the breeding season may begin as early as February or as late as May. Females lay one clutch annually and egg count can be from a half dozen (small, young females) to more than four dozen (females in their prime). Gravid females may nest only a few feet above the water line or may wander 150 or more feet (45.7 m) from the water before nesting. The smooth-shelled, nonglossy eggs are roughly the size and shape of Ping-Pong balls. The emerging hatchlings measure about 1.5 inches (3.8 cm) in straight carapace length. Natural incubation probably takes from three to four months. In captivity, at a consistent 86°F (30°C), incubation lasts about

82 days. The babies were once heavily collected for the pet trade but they are now protected by law in most of the states in which they occur.

Habits: In keeping with their large size, alligator snappers grow rather slowly; if they survive past the vulnerable baby stage they probably attain ripe old age. Certainly they do in captivity. Many properly kept captive specimens have lived to more than twenty—even thirty—in good health.

Although the diet of many hatchling alligator snappers seems to center largely on fish, larger specimens (and probably even wild hatchlings) are more opportunistic. Stomach contents from adults reveal consumption of shellfish, crayfish, snails, other turtles, worms, insects, fish, amphibia, and even some aquatic plants. Captives have readily eaten all of these things plus snakes and raw meat of many kinds.

The ability of the alligator snapper to angle with its tongue process is well documented. This process, when quiescent, is gray and not easily seen, even when the mouth of the turtle is open. Within one or two twitches, however, this double-ended process becomes engorged with blood and turns pink to red.

In comparison with the neck of the widely ranging common snapper, that of the alligator snapper is short and its head proportionally massive. Thus, *Macroclemys* depends mostly on "wait and ambush" techniques while specimens of *Chelydra* more actively seek out their prey.

Although never overly active, *Macroclemys* forages at night.

The Common Snapper

The common snapper *(Chelydra)* has been divided into four (somewhat identifiable) subspecies that range in distribution from southern Canada, southward through the eastern two thirds of of the United States and eastern Mexico and most of Central America to Ecuador in northwestern South America.

Throughout much (if not most) of its range, the common snapper is also referred to as 'gator turtle, probably because of its roughened shell, heavy leg and tail scalation, large head, and readiness to bite when molested.

Appearance: The common snapper may reach a carapace length of about 12 inches (30 cm) and occasionally a few inches more. It is the same mud-brown as the alligator snapper and is darker when young. When viewed from above, the dorsolaterally directed eyes of the common snapper are easily visible; the more laterally directed eyes of the alligator snapper, less easily so. The record size is 19⅜ inches (49.2 cm) in carapace length. One wild specimen weighed in at a whopping 75 pounds (34 kg) and long-term captives have been fattened to 86 pounds (39 kg) (Conant/Collins 1991).

Habits: When submerged in the waters of its home pond, the attitude of the common snapper is often rather benign. It is when this turtle is out of the water, either forcibly or voluntarily, that the trait from which it takes its common name is best observed. Its long neck enables it to reach a target a considerable distance away. When molested, common snappers will snap repeatedly, at times lunging with such force that the whole turtle may skid forward.

Although the head is not as massive as that of *Macroclemys*, the jaws of *Chelydra* are strong. While the wounds from the bite of a large, enraged snapper are entirely lacking in surgical precision, the administration is frightening and the results painful. Just observing the savagery with which the strikes are delivered should be incentive enough to remain well beyond reach of the long neck.

Wide gape, strong jaws, superb camouflage, and a lure-like tongue appendage provide the alligator snapping turtle, Macroclemys temmincki, *with unparalleled angling ability.*

The common snapping turtle is much less restricted in habitat than is *Macroclemys. Chelydra* can be found (at times in numbers) in nearly any pond, lake, pothole, river, or depression that holds water . . . even temporarily. They are even active at very low water temperatures.

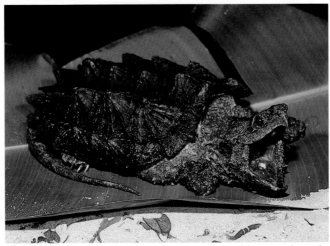

Although not awfully conspicuous at the moment, the tongue-lure of this alligator snapping turtle can be seen.

Like its larger relative *Macroclemys, Chelydra* is also most active at night. Then it actively forages, seeking out fish, amphibians, reptiles (including smaller turtles), carrion, small mammals, and birds. Mollusks, crustaceans, worms, other aquatic organisms, and some plants are also consumed. It was long thought that the plants were merely peripheral, ingested with the snails, shrimp, and other aquatic invertebrates that live among them. However, photographs have now been taken that show large snappers coming out onto land and deliberately grasping fruits and vegetables.

Although certainly not favoring land over water, common snappers are definitely less persistently aquatic than the larger alligator snapper. Common snappers sun not only on emergent snags and stumps, but on banks, sandbars, or leaning tree trunks. Frequently common snappers thermoregulate by floating at the water's surface where their dark color quickly absorbs the sun's warming rays. Adults may also cross wide expanses of land when searching for a new territory.

Breeding: The common snapper usually lays one egg clutch annually. Small young females lay the fewest eggs; large older females, the most. Clutch size varies from eight to more than thirty. Depending on temperature, the incubation time can be as short as 50 days or more than twice that. Specimens that hatch late in the season may overwinter in the nest.

Although nearby sites such as muskrat lodges may be chosen, gravid females may dig and lay their eggs in open sunny areas more than a quarter of a mile from the home pond. One can only wonder how any of the vulnerable hatchlings make it back to the water.

The inch-long (2.5 cm) hatchlings, with three distinct carapacial keels and a noticeably rougher countenance than the adults, are actually rather charming. They resemble dark blobs of mud, in color, and are very retiring.

Both the eggs and hatchlings of the common snapper are vulnerable to predation by ants, raccoons, opossums, herons, snakes, alligators, and a host of other predators.

It was long thought that common snappers were so prolific that their numbers were virtually inexhaustible. Recent results from long ongoing studies have shown this not to be the case at all. In many areas snapper populations have been markedly reduced by nest predation (raccoons and fire ants) and human efforts. This is especially so at the edges of this turtle's range.

Several subspecies or races of the common snapper are recognized. Besides the Florida race, *C. s. osceola*, there are two Latin American races.

Like the alligator snapper, *Chelydra* are hardy and easily maintained as captives. Unlike basking turtle species, neither member of the Chelydridae seems especially dependent upon ultraviolet rays to survive, but each does "sun" themself on occasion.

Other than for egg deposition, snappers of either species do not require a land area if their water is of suitable depth and temperature. For the most part "room temperature"—76 to 82°F (24–27°C)—water is suitable. Slightly warmer (or temporarily slightly cooler) water will not harm these creatures at all. The water should be shallow enough to allow the turtle to breath when its neck is mostly extended. High water quality should always be maintained, with care being taken to remove chlorine and chloramine additives whenever the water is changed. The ammonia content and pH of the water should be controlled by water changes or the pertinent water additive. Chlorine and chloramine additives can be removed with commercial aquarium products from your pet store.

Although hardy throughout their life, and easily kept when young, the large size of an adult of the common snapping turtles makes them specialty species. This is the Florida snapping turtle, Chelydra serpentina osceola.

It is obviously much easier to house hatchlings and juveniles of the Chelydrids in captivity than adults. But fortunately neither the alligator snapper nor the common snapper seem to require a great deal of room to thrive. This should not be construed to mean the creatures should be crowded, but a single small specimen will do well in a ten-gallon (40 L) tank. Of course, should you be fortunate enough to live where the climate is benign enough to allow a permanent shallow in-ground pool or other outside facility, so much the better.

Handling tips: Be careful when handling snappers of either species. Babies can be lifted by merely enveloping them in your hand; larger specimens by grasping them securely by the rear of the shell. Even when this is done properly, the long neck of the common snapper will allow its mouth to nearly reach your fingers.

Larger specimens can be carefully (but securely) grasped by the tail and lifted. The plastron of the turtle *must* be nearest your leg so that the snapping mouth of the turtle is directed *away* from you. Very large specimens are best left alone or, if necessary, lifted with mechanical help. It is nearly impossible for one person to safely handle a viciously striking 60-pound (27 kg) turtle.

No matter how long they have been captives, many snappers of both species will continue to bite if restrained. They also will quickly come to associate the presence of food with that of their keeper and may snap upward in anticipation. Caution should always be foremost in your mind when associating in any manner with these big, powerful, and interesting chelonians.

Mud and Musk Turtles

There are several genera of small to large, highly aquatic, very hardy but seldom-kept turtles classified in this family, the Kinosternidae. They are of New World distribution and may be encountered from New York and the Great Lakes states southward through the northern two thirds of South America.

Most have rugose and strongly keeled carapaces when small. While some retain the roughness and/or keeling throughout their lives, the shells of others smooth and dome with age. So thoroughly aquatic are these turtles that profuse, pattern obscuring algal growths are not uncommon. There is, however, usually little pattern to obscure.

The two genera found in the United States, *Sternotherus*, the musk turtles, and *Kinosternon*, the mud turtles, are closely related. The entire assemblage has been gathered under the single generic name of *Kinosternon* by some authorities. The musk turtles are typified by reduced plastra with a single poorly developed hinge, while the plastra of the mud turtles are proportionately larger and have a hinge at each end of the bridges (the bridges are the areas of shell on the sides which connect the carapace (upper shell) with the plastron (lower shell).

Appearance: None of these turtles is brightly colored, even when a hatchling. The closest that any can come to brilliance is the salmon plastron of the hatchlings of the riverine loggerhead musk turtles, *Sternotherus minor* ssp., or the orangish plastron of the quiet-water common mud turtles, *Kinosternon subrubrum* ssp. The plastral colors quickly fade as these turtles of the eastern United States attain their 4.5 inch (11.4 cm) adult size. Hatchlings of the Central American red-cheeked mud turtle, *K. scorpioides cruentatum*, have variable amounts of red or orange on the sides of the head, which, although fading with growth, usually remains visible throughout the long life of this 8-inch-long (20 cm) turtle.

Several of the musk and mud turtles may have prominent yellow stripes on their faces when young (common musk turtle, *Sternotherus odoratus*, and striped mud turtle, *K. bauri* among them) but these stripes usually fade and often fragment as the turtles age. Besides facial stripes, the striped mud turtle also has three well-defined to obscurely defined yellow(ish) carapacial stripes. These are usually brightest on juvenile specimens.

The closest a mud turtle comes to a light shell color is seen on the olive-yellow to olive-green 5-inch (12.7 cm), yellow mud turtle, *Kinosternon flavescens* ssp., of the central United States. The throat of this last species is much yellower than its shell.

The largest members of this family are from southern Mexico and northern Central America. These are the always-ready-to-bite Mexican giant musk turtles (genus *Staurotypus*) which attain an overall carapace length of about 13 inches (33 cm). These turtles are placed in the family Staurotypidae by some researchers. Babies are occasionally available in the pet trade, and are pleasingly colored in a dark speckled variable gray. Although Mexican giant mud turtles dull in color

Although not brightly colored, common musk turtles, Sternotherus odoratus, *a highly aquatic species of the eastern United States, are easily kept.*

Hatchlings of the giant musk turtle, Staurotypus triporcatus, *are occasionally available in the pet trade. This half-grown specimen has retained more of its juvenile color and pattern than normal.*

as they age, the strongly tricarinate (three keels) carapace of babyhood is retained and may even accentuate as the turtle grows. Of all of the musk and mud turtles, this big, highly adaptable species may be the only one captive-bred in any significant numbers. This is not because they are difficult to breed, but rather, because they are not sought by most advanced hobbyists.

Habits: The rather sedentary lifestyles of the musk and mud turtles make them very amenable to captive conditions. Although often referred to as "nonbaskers," most species actually do seek the sun in one manner or another. Some bask by lying quietly in sun-warmed shallow water with all or part of their carapace exposed. Others may actually climb clear of the water on mudbars or protruding snags or other debris, or actually climb rather

Albino turtles are coveted by collectors. This albino eastern mud turtle, Kinosternon s. subrubrum, *is in the collection of John Lewis.*

high into waterside trees. From such basking platforms startled musk or mud turtles may occasionally drop into boats passing beneath.

Although they are initially shy, musk and mud turtles soon come to recognize that the presence of a person often means that food becomes available. These turtles have strong jaws and can be aggressive toward basking turtles if the latter are housed with them. The jaws of the kinosternids are strong and the injuries caused can be grave.

Although they will do well in spartan quarters, the musk and mud turtles certainly deserve better. Ours are in well-filtered aquariums with rock caves, growing aquatic plants, and an easily accessed, warmed, illuminated, and exposed basking platform. We prefer curved corkbark pieces firmly wedged between the sides of the aquarium for the platform. These turtles are primarily carnivorous. They eagerly accept worms, aquatic insects, crickets, pieces of raw meat and fish, as well as prepared trout, catfish, and cat chows.

Remember also the propensity of these turtles for climbing. You must be certain that they cannot escape by clambering up a filter stem or air hose, or by reaching the top rim of the tank from their basking platform.

Pond Turtles

The four emydine species of turtles of this genus (*Clemmys*) are restricted in natural distribution to the United States and southeastern Canada. They are members of the large family Emydidae. The four are protected by various state laws throughout most of their range. All were once common in the pet trade, but because of their protected status are less frequently seen today.

All species of this genus are bred regularly in captivity, both by zoos and hobbyists. All require a varying degree of winter cooling to cycle reproductively. Although all species have been bred in the deep South, even to the latitude of southern Florida, egg viability seems to drop off after several years of this unnatural heat. This seems especially true of wood turtles.

Three of the four species, the bog turtle, *C. muhlenbergi,* the spotted turtle, *C. guttata*, and the wood turtle, *C. insculpta*, have long been the favorites of hobbyists, and all are now captive-bred in at least small numbers. However, because of their protected status (which varies by state) we urge that you contact the game and fish commissions in the individual states to learn the legalities for keeping these attractive turtles. Many of the states will allow the keeping of *Clemmys*, but not its commercialization.

The Spotted Turtle

A small denizen of wooded ponds and bogs of eastern North America, the spotted turtle attains an adult length of only about 4 inches (10 cm). It seems most common in slightly acidic seeps and ponds that are heavily vegetated with sphagnum. In the early spring, while the weather is still chilly, the males may wander across country roadways in search of females. A few weeks later, egg-laden (gravid) females may wander in the same areas looking for suitable nesting sites. It is at these times that spotted turtles are most often encountered.

Appearance: Hatchlings, which are just over an inch (2.5 cm) in length when emerging from the egg, usually bear just a single yellow spot on each of the large dark gray carapacial scutes. Additional spots usually appear with advancing age and some old specimens are profusely speckled. Orange spots may occur on the neck and head, and the forelimbs and leg axils may vary in color from black to extensively orange.

Habits: Spotted turtles may estivate during the hottest part of the year and hibernate during the cold of winter.

The spotted turtle is primarily an aquatic species and captives should be provided with a water area that is rather extensive, but not necessarily deep. The turtles should be able to access the land area easily and at all points. They will thrive on the diet suggested for semiterrestrial turtle species (see page 26).

The Bog Turtle

A bog and streamside species in the North and a denizen of poorly drained, acidic mountain meadows, pastures, and woodland edges in the South, the bog turtle adult has a shell length of about 3.5 inches (9 cm), and hence is among the smallest of the world's turtle species.

Appearance: In coloration the carapace of the bog turtle is primarily brown to reddish brown. The scutes of the carapace may have poorly defined darker or lighter markings and/or lighter centers. The limbs may be extensively orange or mostly brown. Most specimens have a prominent patch of orange at the rear of the head. This may be in the form of a single large blotch or several smaller ones. Occasional specimens, especially old males, may have the head blotches reduced in size or even lacking.

Bog turtles, "boggies" to those who keep them, are for some reason among the most desired of our native turtle species. Although they are protected in the wild, the offspring of captive specimens find a very eager market. While it is true that these are hardy, pretty, and responsive, there are other turtles that are as hardy, even prettier, and at least as responsive.

Habits: Although well able to swim, boggies more often walk along the muddy bottoms of the shallow acidic streams and bogs that are their homes. They create rather well-defined runways through and between the sphagnum and bog grasses, and females place their small egg clutches in shallow depressions atop marshland grass hummocks. Sadly, the poorly hidden nests are frequently plundered by raccoons, muskrats, snakes, and other predators. Hatchlings are consumed by these and other predatory species, and habitat destruction has noticeably reduced or eradicated entire populations. So secretive are bog turtles that fairly stable populations continue to be discovered even today. However, these discoveries seem more than offset by the dwindling of other populations.

In southwest Florida we provided our bog turtles with a 7-foot (2.1 m) diameter stock watering tank, with a substrate of living sphagnum from 6 to 12 inches (15–30 cm) deep. The turtles often burrowed deeply into this and were difficult to find. However, they seemed to feel secure, ate ravenously, and bred yearly. The stock tank had a drainage hole that was always open. Besides the moisture from the rain, which occasionally left several inches (about 8 cm) of water in the tank, we kept several small, shallow—approximately $10 \times 20 \times 3$ inch ($25 \times 50 \times 7.5$ cm)—plastic water receptacles in the enclosure. The turtles, which were left out of doors year-round, often bred, depositing their eggs in poorly concealed nests in the sphagnum. From one to several clutches of from 2 to 4 eggs were produced yearly by each female. We incubated the eggs indoors.

The diet of these little turtles consisted of worms, pinky mice, and crickets. The turtles occasionally nibbled at fruit, but not enthusiastically. Other breeders have told me that their bog turtles are fed prepared chows exclusively. We tried many different chows and all have been refused.

The Wood Turtles

Once commonly seen over most of its range in the northeastern United States and immediately adjacent Canada, the wood turtle is now considered rare to imperiled. As with other creatures with which we share our world, the causes for population drops are severalfold. Among the most significant of these causes are habitat degradation (including fragmentation), extensive (often illegal) collecting for the pet industry, and increased nest and hatchling predation.

Habits: The wood turtle, often treated as a terrestrial turtle species by many hobbyists, is *very much* a semiaquatic. Although it often wanders and forages in woodlands and brushy meadows far from water, it swims readily, often breeds while in the water, and spends its lengthy period of dormancy in aquatic situations.

Hatchlings (left) of the coveted North American wood turtle, Clemmys insculpta, *are flatter and less colorful than the adults (right). This species is now protected in the wild.*

Bog turtles, Clemmys muhlenbergi, *are now protected from collection throughout their range. The very few, legally available, captive-bred hatchlings (right) command high prices.*

Appearance: The "woodie" is the largest species of the genus. Adults frequently exceed a shell length of 7.5 inches (19 cm). The carapacial color is of some shade of earthen brown, as are the top and sides of the head. The chin, neck, limbs, and tail vary (largely by geographic origin) from pale yellowish green (westerly populations) to brilliant red-orange (easterly populations).

The Pacific Pond Turtle

The fourth member of the genus, the Pacific pond turtle is found in west-central Washington and western Oregon south to almost central California.

Appearance: This is the least colorful of the *Clemmys*—olive gray to olive green with irregular and indistinctly defined lighter and/or darker marblings, reticulations, or radiations. The color of both the soft areas and the shell are quite similar, but the apexes of the limbs tend to be of lighter hue.

Habits: Like the eastern spotted turtle, this is a highly aquatic form, seldom seen away from the water. The Pacific pond turtle is wary, takes fright easily, and dives quickly. This protected species is seen only occasionally in the collections of advanced hobbyists.

Three Exotic "Pond" Turtles with Similar Needs

Turtles in various areas of the world parallel one another, not only in appearance, but in behavior and habitat preferences as well. Three such, which are quite similar to our pond turtles in their captive needs, are the European pond turtle, *Emys orbicularis,* the Asian four-eyed turtle, *Sacalia bealei,* and the Asian pond turtle, *Chinemys reevesi.*

European Pond Turtle

Although the specimens in some populations do get larger, most European pond turtles are adult at between 4.5 and 6.5 inches (11.4–16.5 cm) in shell length. Besides ranging widely in Europe, this little turtle occurs in northern Africa and western Asia.

Appearance: Deep olive-brown, olive-black, or black is the ground color of this prized turtle. Carapacial markings are in the form of tiny dots, spots, or radiations of lighter (often yellow) pigment. The head and limbs, often as dark in color as the carapace, may or may not bear yellow(ish) spots.

Hatchlings are often more dully marked than the adults. Many hatchlings have profuse carapacial speckles of black or dark olive, rather than yellow. Yellow spots are visible on the sides of the head. These often take the form of two irregular stripes on each side.

Breeding: European pond turtles are now bred rather frequently in captivity. Not all females reproduce annu-

The spotted turtle, Clemmys guttata, *is a beautiful pond-dwelling species from eastern North America.*

ally. Some, especially those that have originated from the more northerly portions of the range, produce eggs only biennially or even triennially. Winter cooling seems necessary, to successfully breed even the turtles from southern populations, and it has been suggested that an actual period of hibernation may be necessary to assure fertility in northern specimens.

The Asian four-eyed turtle, Sacalia b. bealei, *was first bred in captivity in the United States by Ellen and Bob Nicol. This specimen is now about half-grown.*

Asian Four-eyed Turtle

This 3.5 to 5-inch-long (8.8–12.7 cm) turtle is superficially like a Pacific pond turtle in appearance, and like the latter often frequents streams and brooks that run through open to rather dense woodland habitats. It ranges over much of southern China and northern Vietnam. If the turtle is purged of parasites and kept in clean facilities, it will thrive in captivity. Because of its predisposition to shell pitting and "rot," clean, basically bacteria-free water is particularly important to the successful maintenance of *S. bealei.*

Appearance: Although the frequently pitted, olive-tan, olive-black to deep brown carapace of *Sacalia bealei* is anything but colorful, the two to four well-defined ocelli (eyespots) on the back of the head (green in males or yellowish in females) and a rose suffusion on the neck and limbs afford this species some attractiveness. The males have the brightest rose on the limbs, a slight plastral concavity, and a longer, thicker tail. The two-spotted form of this turtle, *S. b.* "*bealei,*" is often referred to as Beale's turtle, while the four spotted form, *S. b.* "*quadriocellata*" is usually called the four-eyed turtle.

Habits: Those that we have kept have shown a decided preference for prepared chows (dog, trout and catfish), crickets, and pinky mice. They would occasionally eat apple, grapes, banana (the latter in moderation), and freshly killed minnows. See the section on outdoor caging (page 20) for maintenance suggestions.

Breeding: *S. bealei* has been bred by hobbyists, but only rarely. They seem to require a seasonal (winter) cooling and reduced photoperiod, but not an actual hibernation, to cycle reproductively.

Asian Pond (Reeve's) Turtle

Although it is often referred to as the "Japanese" Reeve's turtle, *Chinemys reevesi* actually has a distribution much greater than just Japan. It is also found over much of China and Korea.

Appearance: The carapace is tricarinate (triple-keeled), with the vertebral keel being the strongest and all keels being best defined on juvenile specimens. Concentric growth rings are retained throughout the turtle's life. Although specimens with shell lengths of more than 9 inches (22.8 cm) have been found, most are much smaller.

The carapace of this inveterate basker may vary from some shade of brown to nearly black. The scute seams are often noticeably darker. Males darken with advancing age. The head is dark with a yellow stripe on each side of the crown and variable reticulations on the cheeks and chin. The limbs are dark. The plastron is brown-blotched yellow.

Breeding: We have had females of 5-inch (12.7 cm) length breed and produce viable eggs. Males are somewhat smaller than adult females and have a heavy, long tail. A weak plastral concavity is sometimes present. Captive breedings supply many hatchlings to the pet trade annually. Females nest several times annually, depositing from 3 to 9 eggs each time. Newly hatched specimens are *tiny*—under an inch (2.5 cm) in length and much longer than wide. Like larger specimens, the babies are very hardy and, if given proper care, grow quickly.

Habits: The Asiatic pond turtle is a hardy, personable species. This is a very cold-tolerant species. We are aware of Asiatic pond turtles being overwintered in outdoor ponds in North Carolina and Virginia. They quickly accept captive conditions and readily associate the presence of a person with the introduction of food to their container. It is an omnivorous species, finding a wide variety of fruit, vegetables, and animal matter entirely acceptable foods.

Latin American Wood Turtles and Asian Wood and Leaf Turtles

The ease with which the various terrestrial and semiterrestrial wood and leaf turtles of Latin America and Asia may be kept makes these turtles appealing to many hobbyists. Although in a different subfamily, the Batagurinae, all are much like the American wood turtles in habits and requirements. These chelonians like large enclosures with shallow ponds. Although Latin American and Asian wood and leaf turtles were once available only as wild-caught specimens, turtle breeders and specialty dealers occasionally have captive-bred and hatched babies of a few species.

Wood Turtles—*Rhinoclemmys*

Like many other terrestrial chelonians, the various *Rhinoclemmys* have a large home range and may wander far beyond those boundaries. They are most active during periods of low barometric pressure and on rainy days. In captivity and when kept as "yard turtles," all may be induced to become active by turning on a lawn sprinkler or otherwise spraying them. Once purged of endoparasites, all these are ideal and hardy captives. As might be expected of subtropical and tropical turtles, all are somewhat cold-sensitive. We have kept them out of doors year-round in Florida, but have provided a warmed turtle house in which all are placed when temperatures dip below the high 40°F (4.4°C).

On cool, sunny days all of these wood turtles bask for long periods. On cool, cloudy days, many remain in their warmed quarters. Although we have seen most of the species kept in facilities as small as 4 × 4 feet (1.2 × 1.2 m), we suggest at least double this ground space, and further recommend that even larger outside facilities be provided for them during suitable weather. We provide one or more large, shallow ponds—3 to 4 inches (7.5–10 cm) deep—in each wood turtle enclosure. Virtually all of the turtles use these readily.

All of the wood turtles that we will discuss here are omnivorous. They will eat all manner of ripe and overripe fruits, some pulpy vegetables, and prepared trout, catfish, dog, and turtle chow. All are able to eat either in or out of the water.

Latin American Wood Turtles

Of the three tropical-American wood turtle species commonly available to turtle hobbyists, one (*R. pulcherrima*) is of moderate size—8 inches (20 cm), more or less—and two (*R. punctularia* and *R. funerea*) must be considered large. Subspecies of *R. punctularia* occasionally exceed 10 inches (25 cm) in length and, with a carapace length of more than 12 inches (30 cm), *R. funerea* is marginally the largest species in the genus. Both *R. pulcherrima* and *R. punctularia* are quite terrestrial, but funerea is predominantly aquatic.

The prettily patterned Central American ornate wood turtle, Rhinoclemmys pulcherrima manni, *is more aquatic than many of its relatives.*

Common names have been coined for all of these species. The subspecies of *R. pulcherrima* are referred to as the Mexican and ornate wood turtles, or, when spoken of collectively, as the painted wood turtles; *R. punctularia* ssp., is known as the spotted-legged wood turtle, and *R. funerea* as the black wood turtle.

In the last three decades, availability of these turtles began with the northernmost representative of this species, the Mexican wood turtle, *R. p. rogerbarbouri*, and ended with the southernmost, the ornate wood turtle, *R. p. manni*, which is readily and inexpensively available today. The two "in between" races, the Guerrero wood turtle, *R. p. pulcherrima* and the Oaxacan wood turtle, *R. p. incisa* were available in the interim.

Appearance: Except for the ornate race, the races of *R. pulcherrima* look very similar. They have a brownish carapace, often with a lighter center on each of the large scutes and a series of thin red stripes on their rather slender, brownish heads. The shells of all

three are rather low and flat, except for that of *incisa* at the southernmost portion of its range, where specimens exhibit some of the characteristics of the more highly domed ornate wood turtle.

The carapacial laminae (or scales) of all retain concentric growth rings. Although the three northern forms are extensively terrestrial, none is at all hesitant to enter water in excess of 12 inches (30 cm). We have found examples of *R. p. rogerbarbouri* in Colima, Mexico, actively foraging in depressions, beneath 2 feet (60 cm) of rain runoff. We have also encountered this turtle wandering in high woodlands far from any water source. Near its point of convergence (where the two subspecies' ranges meet) with the more aquatic ornate subspecies in Nicaragua, *R. p. incisa* tends to also become more aquatic in its habits.

The ornate wood turtle is a semiterrestrial form of variable color. Those in southern Nicaragua (the northern end of the range of this race) can be quite blandly colored, but those from northern Costa Rica are very brightly and beautifully colored. Typically, there are ocelli (eyespots) or reticulations of yellow or dull red on each of the costal scutes and an extensive network of thin bright red lines on the dorsal surface and sides of the head and neck. This is the most highly domed subspecies and we have found it to be most common in and near quiet, shallow waters.

Of the three subspecies of *R. punctularia,* two are seen in the pet trades of the world. Of these, one (*R. p. punctularia)* is commonly seen, and the other (*R. p. diademata*) is only rarely seen. The latter of these may eventually prove to be a full species.

Both of these turtles have spotted forelimbs and dark, rather highly domed carapaces. The two differ only in the color and completeness of the head pattern. The head of *R. p. puntularia*, the nominate form, consists of two rather narrow red (occasionally yellowish) bars, converging but not usually touching anteriorly. These bars begin above the tympanum and terminate above the eye. There is a light spot on each side of the snout and two light spots on the back of the head. This race is found in northeastern South America, from eastern Venezuela and Trinidad southward to Brazilian Amazonas. The subspecies *diademata* (often referred to as the diademed wood turtle) usually has broad yellow head stripes that converge and touch between the eyes. The two posterior crown spots are usually incorporated into the main stripes. This subspecies is restricted in distribution to northwestern Venezuela and northeastern Colombia.

Although wild-collected imported specimens of the nominate form still predominate in the pet markets, captive-bred and hatched babies are being seen with increasing regularity. The few available specimens of diademata are either produced domestically or by European hobbyists. It has been many years since wild-caught specimens have been imported.

The big black wood turtle has become available to the pet market only within the last few years. The available specimens are wild-caught and are being imported from northern Central America.

Although sometimes on the brown side of black (especially when young), there is no question that this is, for the most part, just a big dark turtle in color. The lower jaw is yellowish, spotted with black. This may extend up onto the sides of the face. The limbs are speckled with lighter pigment, and the axillae may be quite light. A light line, often yellow, but sometimes quite fragmented and obscure, is present on the upper side of the head. Additional

The South American wood turtle, Rhinoclemmys p. punctularia, continues to be imported in some numbers for the pet trade.

light lines or reticulations may be present on the side of the head.

The black wood turtle is rather common over much of Central America. Although it may wander quite a

Albinos of the Asian giant wood turtle, Heosemys grandis, are occasionally imported. Normally colored specimens are of some shade of brown.

distance from water, it is often the most common turtle in and around swamps, marshes, oxbows, and slowly moving rivers in forested areas. It basks on protruding snags, logs, and gently sloping banks. It is a strong-jawed omnivore, accepting fruits, herbs, and other greens, as well as animal matter, including carrion.

Asian Giant Wood Turtle

With a record carapace length of just over 17 inches (43.1 cm), *Heosemys grandis* is a grand turtle, indeed.

Appearance: Hatchlings and young specimens are round to oval when viewed from above, but old adults are often quite elongate and may have the shell "roll up" slightly at both anterior and posterior extremities. Normally, the Asian giant wood turtle is another dark turtle. The carapace varies from deep brown through olive-gray to charcoal. The plastron is plain yellow on adults and yellow with dark radiating markings on younger specimens. The head and limbs are grayish. Albinos are not uncommon.

H. grandis might be best described as a semiterrestrial to predominantly terrestrial turtle. Although babies are said by some researchers to be quite terrestrial, those that we have had have spent a good 90 percent of their time in the water and at least half of the remaining 10 percent basking on land at the very edge of their water container. In contrast, Henry, a big adult male that we had, was extensively terrestrial and by choice arboreal. Except to drink, Henry not only shunned all water (except newly forming puddles during rainstorms), but he climbed—and climbed well. He was the most arboreally inclined turtle that we had ever seen. It was not uncommon for us to go into Henry's enclosure and find him firmly wedged, some 5 or 6 feet (1.5 or 1.8 m) above the ground,

between the trunks of the large areca palms that shaded his enclosure. During hot weather, when his metabolism was high, Henry would clamber earthward daily to eat. When the weather was cooler, he might descend only once a week, more often than not to drink rather than eat. But the surest way to get Henry to come to ground was to put a second *Heosemys* in the enclosure. Within minutes, Henry would open his eyes widely (as in disbelief that another giant wood turtle would dare enter his enclosure), pivot until he was nose downward, cascade to earth, and give chase. No other specimen was able to stand ground against Henry—and we had several that closely approached him in size. In defense of his territory, Henry would lunge and bite, chase and straddle, and do everything else that a turtle is able to do to protect his turf. Within minutes the other turtle, whether male or female, would be subdued and, if able, would take flight, always with Henry in hot pursuit. Henry was as adept at climbing the 4-foot (1.2 m) chain-link fence that formed the perimeter of his enclosure as he was at ascending the palm trees. It took us only a few days (and a few escapes) to learn that a 1-foot (30 cm) overhang would be indispensable.

The specimens of this big turtle made available by the pet industry are imported. Specialty dealers and hobbyist-breeders do produce a few captive-bred and hatched babies each year. Even the hatchlings of the giant wood turtle are large. Most measure close to 2.5 inches (6.3 cm) in carapace length at hatching. Both young and adults are omnivorous, readily eating ripe and soft fruits, pulpy vegetables, dark greens (not spinach, please), and prepared foods such as turtle, dog, trout, and catfish chows.

This is an interesting and hardy turtle, but one that roams widely. We consider them "yard turtles." Although they will thrive in smaller terraria and enclosures when young, if cared for properly, they grow quickly, and with that growth will require increasingly large enclosures.

Leaf Turtle

Please note that the Vietnamese leaf turtle, discussed next, is a cool weather turtle species. The recommended temperature for this species is 65 to 75°F (18.3–24°C). We *do* provide a warmed and illuminated basking spot of about 80°F (26.6°C). Most specimens will become inactive at temperatures below 60°F (15.5°C) and become heat-stressed at temperatures above 78°F (25.5°C).

Vietnamese Leaf Turtle

The Vietnamese (also called Asian or black-breasted) leaf turtle, *Geoemyda s. spengleri*, is a marvelous little turtle that has a dismal record in captivity. All available in the pet trade are wild-collected imports, and many, if not most, arrive in the United States stressed and bearing loads of endoparasites. Mouth rot (necrotizing stomatitis) and respiratory illnesses are also often seen in fresh imports. Thus, if this is a species in which you are interested, you must first start out with the healthiest examples available and be prepared to provide even these with the regimens of medications and purges necessary to insure their long-term health.

G. s. spengleri is one of the smallest of the world's turtle species. The largest adults measure only 4.5 inches (11.4 cm). Most are about an inch (2.5 cm) smaller. With a depressed, warm brown, tan, orangish, or yellowish tricarinate carapace (note that all of these are the colors of fallen leaves), healthy *spengleri* are alert and inquisitive. The carapace is deeply serrate posteriorly and less so anteriorly. The head is often colored a shade darker than the cara-

pace, and females bear a yellowish temporal stripe on each side. Females may also have light stripes on the neck. Peach-colored spots are often present posterior to the tympanum, posterior to and below the eye, and on the chin and snout. The large, almost "pop-eyes" of a healthy, well-hydrated specimen have white irides (irises) and impart to this turtle an appearance of intelligence and awareness.

The Vietnamese leaf turtle is a cool-weather species that seems to thrive best when the regimen of care usually used for turtles is reversed. What do we mean by this? Well, bear in mind that we dwell in Florida, a state not known for its cool summer temperatures. But neither does Florida have adversely cold winter temperatures. So, down here, we bring our leaf turtles indoors, into air-conditioned comfort, when the heat of summer truly sets in, and keep them outdoors during the winter months. They thrive! They bask on cool sunny days, remain hidden on both hot and excessively cool days, but are active and seem entirely content at temperatures between 65 and 75°F (18.3–24°C). We have found that although less active during the winter, the leaf turtles do not truly hibernate.

Their quarters are identical to those used for bog turtles—a 7-foot (2.1 m) diameter stock-watering tank containing from several inches (about 8 cm) to a foot (30 cm) of living sphagnum moss as a substrate. Arched pieces of corkbark are provided for hiding areas. Potted Saint-John's-wort and other such low shrubs are contained in the enclosure. These provide visual barriers. A couple of small, shallow plastic water trays—10 × 20 × 3 inches (25 × 50 × 7.5 cm)—are kept filled with clean water. Like the bog turtles, the leaf turtles often soak and defecate in the water, sometimes breed in the water, but seldom remain immersed

Once acclimated, the little Asian black-breasted leaf turtle, Geoemyda s. spengleri, *is hardy and long-lived. It is an alert and active species.*

moss substrate is continually flushed by the rain, or if it seems inordinately dry, by running a garden hose into the tank. The turtles burrow readily and quickly and seem to establish a home territory to which they return after foraging. Although we haven't checked this out, they probably have a series of subsurface tunnels established.

Although they can be a problematic species, leaf turtles now have been kept for more than a decade by experienced turtle hobbyists. Reproductive success with this species was first reported by European hobbyists, and later by their American counterparts. The clutch size is usually only a single, proportionately huge egg—somewhat larger than 1.5 × .75 inches (3.8 × 2 cm)—but females may nest several times a season. The best incubation temperature seems to be 82°F (28°C). Incubation lasts for a few days more than two months.

for long periods. As might be imagined, the water receptacles require frequent cleaning and refilling. The drain hole of the stock tank is always open and the

Box Turtles—
American and Asian

Box turtles are probably the most readily recognized turtles of America. Yes, they are emydine turtles. Despite their tortoiselike lives on land, these highly domed denizens of woodland (eastern subspecies) and brushy prairies (western subspecies) are more closely allied to the painted and spotted turtles than to the tortoises.

Photographs often show the creatures posed among wild strawberries or blackberries, but box turtles actually prefer snails, slugs, worms, and insects for food. Not only do they prefer hard-to-find dietary items, but they can be difficult to acclimate to captive conditions. This seems especially so when "crossovers of habitat" occur. Hobbyists in the western United States often tell us that they consider the eastern box turtles, *Terrapene carolina* ssp., more consistently difficult to acclimate in that area of the country than the native, more arid-adapted western (or ornate) box turtles, *T. ornata* ssp. Eastern hobbyists tell us the westerns are tough for them to acclimate. Thus it seems that captives of the two species (and many subspecies) do best in their respective homelands—where they are preadapted to the vagaries in humidity, temperature, and food items.

Box turtles derive their common name from the ability of the adults to draw the plastron upward against the bottom of the carapace to protect the withdrawn head, limbs, and tail. The cartilaginous hinge is located in the suture between the pectoral and abdominal scales of the plastron. The hinge is undeveloped at hatching, but becomes fully developed by the time the turtle is about one quarter grown. However, during times of plenty, when worms and grasshoppers are abundant and the berry season is in full swing, box turtles may become so corpulent that they are unable to entirely close their plastron.

To accurately sex box turtles, check the secondary sexual characteristics. Certain of these characteristics may vary subspecifically.

• The tail of adult male box turtles is thicker and somewhat longer than that of the female. This holds true for all subspecies.

A plastral hinge (readily visible on this yellow-margined box turtle) allows the various box turtles to close themselves up tightly.

• Adult males of all but the three-toed box turtle have a plastral concavity in the rear lobe of the plastron. This concavity may or may not be present on male three-toed box turtles. It often isn't.
• Adults males of the eastern and Gulf Coast box turtles often have red irides (irises); those of the females are yellow or brown. This is *not* invariable. Rarely females have red eyes, but the irides are usually not the bright red of the eyes of the males. The irides of male three-toed box turtles may be reddish, but often aren't.
• Males of all subspecies tend to have curved, hooklike claws on their hind feet. The claws of the females are straighter.

All races of the eastern box turtle are protected by law in most of the states in which they occur, but despite this protection eastern box turtles seem less common over much of their range today than in past decades. Loss of suitable habitat, including habitat fragmentation, vehicular deaths as the creatures cross highways, collecting for the pet trade, and increased predation by a burgeoning number of predators (ants, raccoons, opossums, armadillos, foxes, and domestic dogs among them) on an ever-decreasing number of box turtle nests have all contributed to the population decline of the eastern box turtles.

The Eastern Box Turtles

Eastern box turtles are divided into subspecies that *usually* have three toes, but sometimes have four toes on the hind feet (three-toed, Mexican, and Florida) and those that usually have four, but sometimes have three toes on the hind feet (Gulf-Coast, Yucatan, and eastern).

Subspecies: There are six recognized subspecies of the eastern box turtle. Four occur in the eastern United States and two in Mexico. Since the two Mexican races, *T. c. yucatana* and *T. c. mexicana,* are seen only in a few zoological collections, we will discuss them no further.

The nominate eastern form occupies the largest range. It is known scientifically as *T. c. carolina* and because many specimens are prettily colored in yellow, oranges, and warm browns (others may be quite drab), it is the subspecies usually depicted on posters and magazine covers. This highly domed, oval turtle is found from northern Florida to Massachusetts and from Michigan to northwestern Mississippi. It is a meadow-edge and open-woodland species. It usually has four toes on the hind feet. Although it is often found near pond and lake edges as well as along woodland and damp meadow streams, the eastern box turtle seldom enters water more than 1 or 2 inches (2.5–5 cm) in depth. If it is forced into or accidentally topples into deep water, it usually bobs on the surface like a cork while paddling clumsily toward the nearest shore.

The southeasternmost representative of the clan is the Florida box turtle, *T. c. bauri.* It is entirely unlike its

Once a prominent pet store turtle, the eastern box turtle, Terrapene c. carolina, *is no longer so. Check the law regarding collecting and keeping this turtle before doing so.*

more northerly cousin in both appearance and color. The black (or nearly black) carapace is elongate and marked with well-delineated radiations of yellow. The rear of the carapace flares outward. The proportionately narrow carapace is very highly domed. There are two yellow lines (these are sometimes fragmented) on each side of the head. This race, which for all intents and purposes is endemic to Florida, is fully protected. You can be reasonably sure that specimens now offered in the pet trade have been gathered in violation of conservation laws. Populations of the Florida box turtle have also been adversely impacted by habitat reduction and fragmentation. The draining of even temporary wetlands adversely affects populations. Damp open woodlands, damp meadows, marshes, and swamp edges are favored habitats of this box turtle. They seldom enter swimming-depth water voluntarily.

The Gulf Coast box turtle, *T. c. major,* often enters water and may be seen walking along the bottom of rather deep canals and waterholes of various kinds. It is the largest of the eastern box turtle subspecies, and although highly domed, has the carapace rather flattened centrally, and the marginals widely flared along the posterior edges. This is a dully colored turtle that is as likely as not to be devoid of strongly contrasting carapacial colors. Old males often have a chalk-white moustache or moustache and sideburns facial markings. In its pure, nonintergraded form, the Gulf Coast box turtle occurs only on Florida's panhandle. However, intergrade specimens showing much Gulf Coast box turtle influence may be encountered from eastern Louisiana to central Georgia. This big box turtle is at home in the moist woodlands and marsh edges of its rather small range. It is protected over most of its range.

Although it is now illegal to collect them from the wild, the Florida box turtle, Terrapene carolina bauri, *is captive-bred in some numbers.*

The three-toed box turtle, *T. c. triunguis*, is the most divergent subspecies. It ranges widely from Missouri and Alabama to eastern Texas and Kansas. Although some specimens may be rather brightly colored, many show a tendency toward a unicolored olive-brown, olive-tan, or horn-colored carapace. Adult males may have a fair amount of red or maroon on the head. Most males lack the plastral concavity so predominant in males of other subspecies.

The courtship of the eastern box turtle is similar to that of many other turtles and tortoises. The male circles and butts females he encounters, nipping at the front of their shell, limbs, and head. If the female is receptive she allows copulation.

A month to six weeks later, the female digs a nest in a root-free area in relatively soft, well-drained soil that receives sunlight for at least part of the day. From two to eight (often four or five) eggs are laid. Multiple clutches are normal. In the northern portion of the range, hatchling box turtles have been known to overwinter in the nest.

Habits: In the north, box turtles hibernate (brumate) for several of the coldest months. There are times when they seem to make surprisingly little effort to seclude themselves. In western Massachusetts, box turtles have been found hibernating with the top of their carapace virtually at ground level. Although the snow does have an insulating quality, the fact that the ground was frozen beneath the turtle and the fact that the turtle emerged from its hibernaculum unscathed indicate other physiological changes occur for protection from the subfreezing temperatures. See HOW-TO: Hibernate Your Turtle, pages 44–45, for guidelines for the hibernation of box turtles in captivity.

All of the eastern box turtles require a high to moderate relative humidity, with the prairie populations of the three-toed species requiring least.

The Western Box Turtles

Much of what we have said for the eastern box turtles applies to the two races of the western box turtle as well. Since the eastern box turtle is largely protected, these two box turtles, the

Because of their secretive habits, hatchling ornate box turtles, Terrapene o. ornata, *are not often encountered in the wild.*

vividly marked ornate, *T. o. ornata* and, more rarely, the pallid desert *T. o. luteola*, have become the types most frequently seen in the pet trade of the United States and Europe. They are pretty but seem even more difficult to acclimate and establish in captivity than their eastern relatives.

Western or eastern? Differentiating between the western and eastern box turtles isn't difficult. At first, the ornate box turtle may be mistaken for a Florida. However, the dark carapace of the ornate box turtle is not so highly domed; in fact it is flattened centrally. Additionally, the prominent radiating yellow lines of its carapace seem heavier and not quite as precisely delineated as the carapacial markings of the Florida box turtle. Rather than bearing two prominent light lines on each side of the head like the Florida box turtle, the head of the ornate box turtle is usually prominently spotted. The dark plastron of the ornate box turtle is heavily patterned with bold light lines; the plastron of the Florida box turtle is light, occasionally with a few dark markings. If present, these markings are best defined along the scute sutures and on the anterior lobe of the plastron.

Desert or ornate? The ground color of the desert box turtle is considerably lighter than that of the ornate. Additionally, the light carapacial markings of the desert subspecies are thinner and more numerous, but usually do not contrast sharply with the ground color. All markings are best defined on young specimens; old specimens may be an almost unicolored yellowish tan or horn-color.

Range: As mentioned earlier, the two races of the western box turtle are creatures of open plains, prairies, and related scrub and low brush thickets. Although the desert race inhabits the driest habitats, it often chooses irrigated areas and the environs of waterholes and river edges for its microhabitat. *T. o. ornata* occurs in patches of suitable habitat from Indiana and South Dakata to the lower Rio Grande Valley. *T. o. luteola* ranges over much of far western Texas, westward to New Mexico and southward across the Rio Grande into adjacent Mexico.

Breeding: Unlike the reproductive strategies of the eastern box turtles, which involve much "courtship," the breeding sequence of the western box turtle is often more straightforward. When a male western box turtle encounters a receptive female (pheromone production quite probably plays a considerable role in determining receptivity) he often merely scurries forward and mounts her. Some males will stop to sniff the rear margin of the female's shell, to redetermine receptivity. Some males will sniff and butt the female, but many, especially captives, dispense with all courtship formalities.

The male ornate box turtle has the innermost toe enlarged and angled differently from the others. This helps him in positioning during breeding. The nesting sequence and clutch size is similar to that of the eastern box turtle.

Except in the lower Rio Grande valley, where the ornate box turtle is active for all but a few days of the year, both races of the western box turtle hibernate for the several months of winter.

The Asian Box Turtles

Certain turtles don't fit conveniently into either the aquatic or the terrestrial sections. Such are the several Asian box turtles, which despite moderate to high carapacial doming, are often as at home in water as out of it. Since all have plastral hinges and can close every bit as tightly as the American box turtles, we have decided to discuss them here. The generic name of *Cistoclemmys* has been suggested for several members of this genus. The

The flatter carapace and lack of a dark face stripe differentiates this ornate box turtle from the Florida box turtle.

change has not yet been well accepted, so we will use the older designation of *Cuora*.

The most commonly seen and inexpensive of the Asian box turtles is *Cuora amboinensis*. Despite a range extending well beyond the confines of Malaya, this species is frequently referred to as the Malayan box turtle. It is actually found, besides in Malaya,

Although having a highly domed carapace, the Malayan box turtle, Cuora amboinensis, *is persistently aquatic.*

69

from the Philippines to the Nicobars and from Vietnam through Thailand. It is one of the most aquatic and least colorful of the genus. The smoothly rounded carapace of an adult varies, by population, from somewhat flattened to highly domed, and is black in color. The plastron is yellowish, as are the soft body parts; the limbs are dark. The dark head and neck are prominently striped with yellow. The uppermost pair of stripes (one on each side) converge on the tip of the snout. The hatchlings are dark and have three dorsal keels (tricarinate). This is a rather slow-moving, shy turtle. Imports are quick to withdraw into the safety of their shell and may remain immobile and withdrawn for long periods. Although most are considerably smaller, the Malayan box turtle does occasionally attain a shell length of 8 inches (20 cm).

Habits: Captives of this quiet, inoffensive turtle seem quite omnivorous. They eat all manner of nonnoxious water plants, romaine, escarole, and other dark leafy vegetables, a fair variety of fruit, snails, worms, crayfish, and prepared foods such as trout, catfish,

and dog chows. Although it has been elsewhere stated that the species is preferentially herbivorous, even our fresh imports have accepted animal matter as readily as plants.

Breeding: If sexually mature and cycled through a natural photoperiod, females of the Malayan box turtle may deposit several sets of two eggs at about two-week intervals. This species can be tough to sex. Some males have a plastral concavity. About the only invariable is the proportionately longer and heavier tail of sexually mature males.

The yellow-margined box turtle is the most popular of the Asian box turtles with hobbyists. It is *Cuora flavomarginata*. Most specimens available in the pet trade are wild-collected and imported from China. Determined by availability, the price of this species fluctuates wildly. Although they are currently rather inexpensive and readily available, we have seen prices of more than $100 during periods of scarcity.

Habits: This is a colorful and, once acclimated, outgoing and hardy species of box turtle. We have had a number of specimens for many years. They wander around in the fenced backyard, sharing chow and water with the dogs and other species of box turtles. However, fresh imports are very shy and may remain tightly closed within their shells for hours. We have found all to be most active during rainstorms and barometric pressure drops that accompany passing frontal systems.

Appearance: The shell of this basically terrestrial species is moderately to highly domed and the concentric growth rings remain prominent, unless physically worn from the shell by abrasion. The carapacial color of the yellow-rimmed box turtle is somewhat variable—brown, olive-brown, or black. There is usually a rather prominent vertebral stripe and the marginals are yellow on their undersides; from the yellow

The brightly colored head of the Asian yellow-margined box turtle, Cuora flavomarginata, *contrasts nicely with the dark carapace color.*

rim both common and specific names are derived. The head is very prettily colored. The olive-gray to olive-brown of the crown is separated from the yellow-green of the cheeks by a yellow (sometimes greenish yellow) stripe that is thinly delineated by a darker edging. The lower cheeks and chin shade to a pale peach to brighter yellow. The legs are dark, the axillae yellowish. This is another turtle species that is very difficult to sex. The tail of *both* sexes is short, but that of the male is comparatively wider at the base. The posterior lobe of the male's plastron is straight in side view and rounded when viewed from above. The corresponding plastral lobe of the female is *slightly* more angular and the posterior tip may curve slightly upward when viewed from the side. Most of our adults are between 4.5 and 5.5 inches (11–14 cm) in carapace length.

This is an omnivorous turtle species. Ripe and overripe fruits, worms, cat foods, mice, and nearly any other edible thing are eagerly consumed.

Breeding: Our female yellow-margined box turtles have several nestings annually of either a single egg or a pair of eggs. The nests are very shallow and the layings are separated by from 10 to 18 days. In Florida we have always allowed nature to take its course and find hatchlings in the yard from late summer to very late fall; we make no effort to provide heat or additional lighting for the turtles. Here the cycling and nesting are all accomplished naturally.

About 15 years ago a newly available Asian box turtle took the American pet industry by storm. Until then virtually unknown, or at least unseen, the "newcomer" was the Indochinese box turtle, *Cuora galbinifrons*. Remarkably variable, always beautiful, and often stressed and delicate, the initial imported specimens commanded a price of several hundred dollars each.

Although it can be difficult to acclimate, the subtle beauty of the Indochinese box turtle, Cuora galbinifrons, *makes the effort to do so well worthwhile.*

They are now selling at less than $50 each. The beauty of this turtle is indicated by an alternate American name—"hundred-flower turtle." This seems a literal translation of one of several Vietnamese names applied to the species. Many dealers continue to list *C. galbinifrons* as the "three-hill box turtle," a reference to geographic origin.

Appearance: Actually, the Indochinese box turtle is a two-toned species, and neither of those colors—buff (or tan) and brown—is bright. It is the variable design of their combination that makes this turtle species so attractive. One of the more frequently seen combinations creates a deep brown and variably reticulate dorsal area. There is often a buff vertebral stripe dividing the brown. The brown extends downward, involving about the top third of the costal scutes. The marginals are the same deep brown, darkest on the front bottom corner and the very top of each scute. Sunburst radiations of brown connect the top marking with the bottom. Between these dark areas the costal scutes are a warm tan, cream, horn, or buff. They may be immaculate (without colored spots) or variably marked with dark pigment. The head, neck, and limbs are tannish. The head may be reticulated or flecked with darker pigment. Adults range from 6.5 to 8 inches (16–20 cm) in carapace length. This terrestrial turtle is known to dwell in high elevation woodlands in Vietnam and surrounding areas. The specimens now available in the pet trade of the world have been imported from Vietnam. Most of them are seriously dehydrated and heavily parasitized when they arrive in the United States. These problems *must* be addressed immediately.

Habits: We have found newly imported *C. galbinifrons* to be the shyest of the genus. The slightest external movement will cause them to withdraw and close their plastron tightly. Once withdrawn, it is not unusual for them to remain so for the better part of an hour. When they finally do begin to open, any disturbance will cause reclosure. They are, therefore, difficult turtles to medicate orally, and nearly as difficult to entice to feed. We found, quite by accident, that live half-

grown white mice may induce reluctant feeders to eat. While feeding mice to some newly imported keeled (jagged-shelled) box turtles, *Pyxidea mouhotii*, one of the mice crawled over into the enclosure of the Indochinese boxes. Two females that had never before eaten for us gave immediate chase, quickly caught, killed, and consumed the mouse. Prekilled mice were immediately incorporated into the proffered diet and were eagerly accepted by all members of the group. Once feeding, the turtles branched out to night-crawlers, canned and kibble-type cat food, and sweet fruits.

Breeding: Although hardy once acclimated, we have not yet seen breeding activity amongst our *galbinifrons*. Neither have we been able to learn of reproductive success in other collections. However, as we continue to learn more about the needs and preferences of this turtle, and as we incorporate our findings into our husbandry regimens, captive *C. galbinifrons* should feel increasingly at home. Captive reproduction is almost sure to follow.

The Indochinese box turtle does not seem particularly temperature-sensitive. As with all its congeners except *C. amboinensis* (which we protect from cool weather), we leave *galbinifrons* in its outside enclosures year-round in Florida. During the passage of cold fronts the Indochinese box turtles push themselves beneath piles of leaves, and none has ever shown indications of distress following its emergence. Temperatures in our area occasionally drop to freezing.

Another *Cuora* occasionally seen in the pet trade is the highly aquatic, low-domed, and elongate Chinese three-striped box turtle, *Cuora trifasciata*. At one time it was a commonly imported species, but is, at the moment, somewhat less so. It has been bred in captivity.

Although not brightly colored, once acclimated, the Asian keeled box turtle, Pyxidea mouhotii, *is alert, active, and agile.*

Appearance: In coloration the carapace of this turtle varies from brown to terra-cotta. It is a tricarinate (three-keeled) species. A dark stripe often parallels each keel, with the vertebral stripe being invariable.

Habits: Although it seems primarily carnivorous, captives will occasionally accept pieces of ripe peach, apples, bananas, and berries. The base diet of our specimens is a mixture of trout, catfish, and dog chows. This is a very hardy turtle species. Adults can be aggressive toward other turtles, both of their own and other species.

Breeding: This species often breeds while under water.

The keeled box turtle, *Pyxidea mouhotii,* is the last of the box turtles we will mention. Conventional wisdom has it that this is an almost entirely herbivorous species, and they *do* consume vegetation. But for a display of agility almost unparalleled in turtledom, put a small mouse in this turtle's pen, then stand back and watch. The pursuit of the rodent by this curious little turtle will probably be nearly instantaneous, and with shell held high from the ground, the turtle will match the rodent's every move, eventually overtaking and killing it. This perfected response would seem more that of a predator—not an expected response from a reptile that is primarily herbivorous.

Appearance: There is nothing colorful about keeled box turtles. Head, limbs, tail, and carapace are rather uniformly some shade of brown. Color strays toward tan on some specimens or toward russet on others, but there is always a brown overtone.

The plastron, also brown, usually bears a dark smudge in each scute. The plastron is smaller than the bottom of the carapace, thus does not close as tightly as the plastra of certain other species.

The flattened dorsal area and flattened slanting costal scutes give the keeled box turtle a characteristic shape. If the turtle at which you are looking is shaped like a rhomboid when viewed head on, it is a keeled box turtle.

The alternate common name—jagged-shelled turtle—comes from the jaggedly serrate posterior edge of the carapace.

Habits: Offsetting their somber color, once acclimated, keeled box turtles are among the most alert and trustful turtles. A pair that we have had for many years will trail us about their pen. *Pyxidea* ranges widely in Vietnam, Burma, and adjacent China. The specimens currently available in the American pet trade are imported from Vietnam.

Let's Talk Box Turtle Diet and Housing

Box turtles are popularly thought to be among the most ideal of pet turtles. And they are—after they have been acclimated to captive conditions. One of the things that makes box turtles so desirable to so many people is the fact that they eat a wide range of food. This, too, is true. Box turtles are not entirely frugivorous, nor are fruits even the favorite food of many specimens. This can easily be seen by the initial attitude of many new captives toward fruit. They'll walk all around it, some may even sniff it—but they won't eat it!

But if you want to induce a recalcitrant newly acquired eastern box turtle to feed, try a night crawler. The box turtle will almost jump on the worm in its haste to feed! Western box turtles are less enthusiastic about worms, but are usually instantaneously interested in—are you ready for this?—dung beetles (oh yes, and crickets and locusts). Once the turtle is feeding, it can be weaned over to canned cat foods and various fruit, berries, and mushrooms. Treats of worms and crickets will always be appreciated though.

Although we have kept box turtles indoors, usually loose in a room (rarely in a large caged area), we have always considered these creatures better suited for outdoor existence. To this end we have constructed cages for each species and subspecies that we have kept, that we may better provide for the needs of each. No matter at what latitude you live, if you can control humidity (high for eastern and Asian box turtles, low for westerns), box turtles will thrive out of doors during summer weather. However, how you prepare the turtles for winter will vary by species and latitude. Asian, Gulf Coast, Florida, and southernmost individuals of other species and subspecies will require no period of hibernation, thus, at northern latitudes, these are best housed indoors for the winter. However, if you live in the lower Rio Grande valley or peninsular Florida, modifications can be made which will enable you to keep the turtles outside year-round. They may be inactive for a few days during the passing of strong cold fronts. Again, we refer you to our comments on hibernation, beginning on page 43.

Map and Sawback Turtles

Riverine Gems

The emydine map turtles of the species *Graptemys* are remarkable for their extreme sensitivity to unclean water conditions and for the size differentiation between the males and the females. Adult females can attain but rarely exceed a 10-inch (25 cm) carapace length. The females also tend to fade in color and pattern. Males, on the other hand, are adult at about 4.5 inches (11 cm) in length—some may attain 6 inches (15 cm)—and retain the brilliancy of the hatchlings.

The dozen species are found in river systems and nearby ponds and lakes of the central and eastern United States. The greatest concentration of species, several of them of endangered status, occurs in the river systems of Alabama, Florida, Louisiana, and Mississippi.

Graptemys, which are basking turtles, are informally divided by appearance into the "narrow-headed" and the "broad-headed." Some of the smaller, "narrow-headed" species are reasonably hardy throughout their lives if kept in clean filtered water. The adult males and hatchlings and juveniles of both sexes of even the big, broad-headed species may be maintained with relative ease. The importance of clean filtered water to the health of the map turtles cannot be overemphasized. Without nearly absolute cleanliness, map turtles are very prone to disfiguring and potentially fatal shell lesions.

Appearance: The map turtles derive both common and generic names from the intricate carapacial markings. These light lines, forming circles, blotches, and reticulations, are best defined on the hatchlings and juveniles. However, of the species in which the females attain great size, the smaller adult males also are often prominently marked.

Babies of four forms of *Graptemys* are frequently offered in the pet trade. Map turtles of several additional species, including endangered forms, are rather regularly offered by specialty reptile dealers. (See comments on the laws governing the sale of endangered turtles, page 24).

Habits: Map turtles are highly carnivorous. The diet of the several narrow-headed forms and the juveniles

With advancing age, the females of some map turtles (this is the Escambia map turtle, Graptemys ernsti*) develop enlarged heads that allow them to crush and eat mollusks and crustaceans.*

Although inhabiting brackish coastal areas and of a different genus, the diamond-backed terrapin, Malaclemys terrapin *ssp., is closely allied to the map turtles.*

and males of the broad-headed forms consists largely of aquatic insects, small crayfish, snails, and other such water-dwelling fare. The diet of the females of the various broad-headed map turtles changes as these turtles mature. Adult female common, false, Alabama, Barbour's, Escambia, and Pascagoula map turtles develop conspicuously enlarged heads, strengthened jaw muscles, and flattened crushing (alveolar) plates behind the mandibles. Adult females of these six map turtle species feed largely on crayfish, gastropods, and bivalves. Needless to say, a bite by an adult female of any of these forms would be unpleasant. Providing the necessary diet in captivity is difficult.

Map turtles, as a group, are highly aquatic and extremely wary. Preferentially map turtles bask regularly on protruding snags, brush, and sandbars that are either water-surrounded or spacious, peninsulalike expanses.

The taxonomy of many of the map turtles is controversial. This is especially true in the Ouachita/false/Mississippi map turtle group. Scientific designations may vary in other listings.

When attempting to identify these mentioned map turtles, one must consider the following:
• What is the arrangement of the spots on the head?
• Is there a vertical crescent?
• Are these spots behind the eye?
• What is the shape of the spots?
• Are the spots vertically or horizontally oriented?
• Are spots present on the mandibles?

To make a difficult task even more difficult, where ranges of subspecies (species?) of map turtles overlap, intergradation (hybridization?) occurs. To even attempt identification of some of these specimens, it is necessary to have an up-to-date field guide in hand, and to extrapolate as well.

The Mississippi map turtle, *G. (pseudogeographica) kohni,* is the

The Mississippi map turtle, Graptemys kohni, *is the species most commonly available in the pet trade.*

most commonly offered of the baby map turtles. In this species the plastron is more prominently and intricately patterned than the carapace. Mississippi map turtles are best identified by the presence of a big yellow (sometimes fragmented) crescent behind each eye. Even if incomplete, no other head stripes extend past it to the eye. This pretty turtle is considered a full species, *G. kohni,* by some researchers.

The very similar false map turtle, *G. p. pseudogeographica*, is also frequently seen in the pet trade. Rather than a crescent, the false map turtle has an often transverse elongate spot or two behind each eye, but some of the lower head stripes reach the eye. There are no prominent light spots on the mandibles of either of these map turtles.

The Ouachita map turtle (variously *G. o. ouachitensis* ssp. or *G. pseudogeographica ouachitensis*) has a roughly rectangular longitudinal blotch

behind the eye, a light spot beneath each eye, and a light spot, posteriorly on each side of the lower jaw. The very closely allied Sabine map turtle, which may be referred to as *G. pseudogeographica sabinensis* by some authorities and *G. ouachitensis sabinensis* by others, is nearly identical, but the postocular blotch is oval rather than rectangular.

These map turtles all have a low but well-defined vertebral keel.

The common map turtle, which occurs over much of the same range as the previous four, has an irregular blotch behind the eye, a widened yellow line behind the mouth, and only a weakly *keeled* carapace.

Sawbacks: Three (with a recently discovered fourth species waiting to be formally described) closely allied small map turtles occur in the major river systems of Mississippi, adjacent Louisiana, and Alabama.

Appearance: The vertebral keel of these three is so accentuated that they are usually referred to as sawbacks. The center rear of the first three vertebral scutes projects strongly upward, producing a serrate appearance when viewed from the side. Of the three, the ringed, *G. oculifera*, and the yellow-blotched, *G. flavimaculata,* are officially endangered species in the United States. A very few captive-bred and hatched babies are occasionally available at prices that reflect this scarcity. Somehow, the remaining species, the black-knobbed sawback, *G. nigrinoda* ssp., (represented by two races) has eluded federal listing so far and is rather regularly seen in the pet trade each spring and summer. This is a small and beautiful turtle (see photo, page 110) that is restricted in distribution to three river systems in southern Alabama. Females of all of these species attain about 7.5 inches (19 cm) in shell length and the males about half that.

It is from the conformation of its vertebral keel that the black-knobbed sawback takes its name. The black vertebral projections are large and bluntly rounded. We have watched this species basking on projecting snags on the Black Warrior River (Alabama) and have been amazed by how alert and unapproachable these turtles were. While, with some care, we were able to get close enough to photograph the yellow-blotched and ringed sawbacks, we never once succeeded in approaching *G. nigrinoda* close enough for photographing.

One of the very prettiest of the map turtles is the southeastern Texas Cagle's map turtle, *G. caglei*. It is another of the narrow-headed insect eaters and is brilliantly and intricately marked. It is now being captive-bred in very small numbers. Cagle's map turtle is similar in size to the black-knobbed.

While most turtles of this genus will readily accept prepared foods, they become truly animated when live food such as crickets is occasionally provided. Although certainly very different in food value from the larvae of the caddis and mayflies for which these turtles would usually forage, gut-loaded crickets (those which have been fed upon chicken starter mash or a mixture of fruit and vegetables) seem to be a welcome addition to a balanced diet that includes trout, catfish, and reptile chows.

Painted Turtles

Pet Store Favorites

If we were to divide the United States into quadrants, only the southwestern quadrant would be devoid of painted turtles. One or more of the four races, or subspecies, of these beautiful emydine turtles occur in each of the other three quadrants. Painted turtles, *Chrysemys*, are rather closely allied to the big basking sliders and cooters of the genera *Pseudemys* and *Trachemys*.

However, painted turtles (especially the young) seem to consume less plant material than the essentially herbivorous cooters and sliders. Painted turtles become more herbivorous with advancing age. Babies eat snails, tiny leeches and worms, aquatic insects, slow, dying, or dead fish and other carrion, and some aquatic plant material. Adults seem to reverse this, first seeking plant material to eat, and secondarily ingesting animal matter. Captives thrive on a combination of prepared foods (various turtle diets, trout chow, catfish chow, and dog chow) and leafy greens. Whenever possible we gather up armfuls of aquatic vegetation (*Vallisneria, Elodea, Hydrilla*, and the like) and dump it into the turtle tank as a treat. It doesn't last long.

Like the sliders and cooters, the painted turtles are inveterate baskers. They become active each spring soon after most of the ice has melted from their ponds and remain active until the ice has virtually mantled their ponds again the following winter. We have seen them in New England basking, three deep, on a leaf-strewn ice floe in the strengthening rays of an early March sun. We have even seen half-grown painted turtles through transparent winter ice as the turtles walked upstream against a fair current at the mouth of a pond's feeder stream.

Painted turtles are hardy beasts, and they will thrive as captives if provided with clean water, suitable basking areas, and nutritious foods. They can withstand warmth, cold, and all the range between. Northern painted turtles can overwinter outside in all of the northern United States and southern Canada, if hibernating provisions are made, and if their pond does not freeze all of the way to the bottom. Both northern and southern specimens can be wintered outside in our southern tier states with little or no preparation. The important thing to remember is that they be allowed to thermoregulate and to feed when so inclined.

Of the four subspecies of painted turtles, it is the southern, *C. picta dorsalis* (of the Mississippi drainage south of Illinois) and the western, *C. p. bellii* (of northern Oklahoma and Illinois west to Oregon and British Columbia) that are now most frequently seen in the pet trade.

The southern painted turtle, identified by a prominent orange vertebral stripe, is the smallest—to 5.5 inches (14 cm)—of the four races. The western painted turtle, which occasionally exceeds 9 inches (22.8 cm) in carapace length (but is usually smaller) is the largest race. It has a netlike reticulum of light (sometimes red) lines on the carapace and a red plastron that bears a light-centered dark central blotch with arms that

The western painted turtle, Chrysemys picta bellii, *is one of the most colorful of all turtle species.*

follow the scute seams, sometimes to the edge of the plastron.

The two remaining races, the eastern—6 inches (15.2 cm), and the midland—to 5.75 inches (14.6 cm), are somewhere between the other races in size. It can be hard to differentiate between the eastern and midland painted turtles. This is especially so in areas where intergradation is common. The range of the eastern painted turtle, *C. p. picta,* pretty much follows the eastern seaboard from Nova Scotia to central North Carolina, where it then follows the Piedmont and mountain provinces inland to central Georgia. The midland painted turtle is found essentially west of the eastern turtle's range, from Canada southward to Tennessee, and dipping down to Alabama and northeastern Georgia. The eastern painted turtle has an unmarked or unpatterned, solid-colored plastron and the carapacial scutes are bordered with olive and arranged pretty much in straight rows. The midland painted turtle, *C. p. marginata,* has a

solid lengthwise dark blotch on the plastron (no outward extending arms) and the vertebrals are not in line crossways with the costal scutes.

A female painted turtle (especially the most northerly ones) may not lay eggs every year. On years that she does lay, she may produce several clutches of from 4 to 10 (rarely to 18) eggs. The interval between nestings is from two to three weeks (longer if weather is unseasonably cool and metabolism is slowed). The nests are several inches (about 8 cm) deep, easily accommodating all of the eggs with ample room left for a thick earthen cover. The nests are dug in open, sunlit areas. Somewhat less than three months is required for incubation. Late hatchlings have been known to overwinter in the nest.

We consider painted turtles excellent pets, especially in garden pools. If kept in clean, quasi-natural conditions, their lifespan may exceed fifteen years. The known record for a captive is just over twenty years.

80

Sliders, Cooters, and Red-Bellies

True Hobby Favorites

Back in the 1940s and 1950s, there were 5 & 10 cent stores, each with a pet counter on which was a flat "goldfish bowl." In the bowl was an inch or two (2.5–5 cm) of water and about 50 very crowded silver-dollar-sized turtles. Most of these little turtles were red-eared sliders or river cooters, all clad in shells of variable green. We thought them wonderful then, even though we knew so little about them.

Slider? Cooter? What do these names mean? The first one is easily explained. It refers to the tendency these turtles have when they are startled—they *slide* into the water. Cooter was derived from "kuta," a word of African origin that means turtle. The name arrived on American shores in the days of slavery.

The Sliders

The best known of the sliders is the red-eared slider, *Trachemys scripta elegans*. It is just one of fourteen subspecies of the slider complex, of which the yellow-bellied slider, *T. s. scripta,* is the nominate form. A third race found in the United States is the Cumberland slider, *T. s. troosti,* of Tennessee's Cumberland Plateau. The Cumberland slider is almost unknown in the pet trade. Eleven additional forms may be found in Latin America. Of these subspecies, several are sporadically to regularly seen in the pet trade.

The red-ear was originally the Mississippi drainage representative of the clan, while the yellow-belly occurred in the Southeast. Both of these now intergrade extensively, and the red-eared slider—the most commonly kept pet turtle in the world—may now be found acclimated and established in most of our contiguous 48 states as well as in Hawaii, Australia, Japan, France, and many other entirely unnative geographic locations.

Appearance: Red-eared sliders regularly attain a shell length of 9 inches (22.8 cm). More rarely they may near 11 inches (27.9 cm) in length. The plastron of the red-eared slider bears prominent ocelli, and the common name is derived from the broad red

Although still expensive, albino red-eared sliders, Trachemys scripta elegans, *are now frequently available.*

The yellow-bellied slider, Trachemys s. scripta, *is an abundant southeastern United States species.*

stripe behind each eye. That same reddish stripe is shared by virtually all of the tropical forms, but not by the other two United States races. In fact,

Trachemys scripta chichiriviche *is a red-eared slider from northern Venezuela.*

rather than a stripe, the yellow-bellied slider has a bright yellow blotch behind each of its eyes. This conspicuous marking is brightest in juveniles and female specimens, but is an excellent field mark when present. The plastron of the hatchling yellow-bellied sliders bears ocelli anteriorly but is usually immaculate posteriorly. The plastral markings fade with advancing age and are often present on older examples as poorly defined dusky smudges.

The green shell color of all subspecies fades with age. It is retained most strongly by female specimens. Males' shells darken with age and may appear to be mostly or entirely black. One or more strains of albino red-eared sliders have been developed and are now commonly available. Even more recently, interestingly colored forms called "pastels" have become available. Although several of the breeders of these variations claim otherwise, it seems probable that these colors are the result of temperature manipulation during incubation. Certainly many of the pastels have fragmented shell scutes and curiously truncated snouts, both of which characteristics are associated with improper incubation temperature.

The Cooters

The several cooters are most commonly encountered in waters that are moving, no matter how slowly. The two most commonly seen kinds are the hieroglyphic river cooter, *Pseudemys concinna hieroglyphica,* and the Peninsula cooter, *P. floridana peninsularis.* The latter is more apt to be in nonmoving waters than the former. Both of these cooters grow to more than 15 inches (38.1 cm) in length.

As hatchlings, both the hieroglyphic river cooter and the Peninsula cooter are little green turtles with variable yellow markings on head, neck, limbs, and carapace. The former, a resident of the rivers systems of the Gulf drainage, tend to have the carapacial markings as multitudinous rings (circles). The plastron is reddish with dark markings following the scute seams. With growth, the color of this turtle fades to grayish and the rings of babyhood fade. Instead, the carapace of the adult is marked with light dots, dashes, circles, spirals, and bars—hieroglyphics, if you will. The most consistent of these markings is a well-defined letter "C" on the second carapacial scute. The plastron retains the dark seam markings but fades to pale yellow.

The most definitive markings of the Peninsula cooter, at any age, are a pair of light yellow hairpins, the closed end behind each eye. The carapace of the adult is dark, with broad well-defined to obscure lighter markings. The heaviest of the light markings are in the form of vertical bars. The markings of the hatchlings are not well-defined, but those on the costal scutes are usually vertically oriented. The plastron of both hatchlings and adults is an unmarked yellow.

One of the prettiest of cooters offered in the pet trade is the Florida red-bellied turtle, *Pseudemys nelsoni.* This is another large species, often attaining a carapace length of 12 inches (30 cm) and rarely more than 14 inches (35 cm).

The babies are green, with head stripes that are less numerous than those of their congeners. The shaft of a yellow arrowlike marking lies between the eyes, with the point on the snout. The plastron of the babies is usually some shade of orange (rarely more yellow than orange). Adults darken but often develop a broad vertical orange or red bar on each costal scute. The plastron may fade to yellow centrally but usually retains orange edges.

Intergrading (interbreeding of sub-species) and hybridizing (interbreeding of species) can make identification

Because of its intricate markings, the northern South American Trachemys scripta callirostris *is often called the "ornate" red-eared slider.*

of these big basking turtles even more confusing than normal. Consider *all* characteristics on problematic specimens.

Sliders, cooters, and kin, including the closely allied painted turtles of the genus *Chrysemys*, are highly aquatic

Termed "pastels," the malformed shells of these aberrantly colored red-eared sliders suggest that they were produced by using incorrect incubation temperatures.

The ocelli on the submarginal plates identify the Florida cooter, Pseudemys f. floridana.

basking turtles. They forage and swallow while in the water, utilizing both sight and smell to find foodstuffs. The adults of all are quite omnivorous, consuming quantities of the various eel-grasses, *Hydrilla, Elodea* and other aquatic vegetation, fruits and leaves of terrestrial plants that drop into the water, plus worms, snails, small fish, fish eggs, tadpoles, frogs, and carrion. The hatchlings and juveniles are more carnivorous. Captives eat all of the above items, plus trout, catfish, dog, cat, and turtle chows, and vegetables such as romaine, escarole, kale, and melons, and some banana. Iceberg lettuce is of no benefit to these or any other turtle. Feed your pet turtles the dark green lettuces mentioned above.

If kept indoors, babies of these species can live in filtered aquariums that are prettily planted and landscaped. With growth, the turtles begin to consider their plantings as food.

Adults are best kept as garden pool turtles. Those from the more temperate areas of the United States are quite cold-tolerant; tropical races and those from the Florida peninsula and lower Rio Grande valley are less so. Warmth-adapted species should be brought into an indoors aquarium during periods of cold weather. If protected from freezing and offered hibernation facilities, the more northerly forms can be kept out year-round in most areas.

Since basking is both psychologically and physiologically important to turtles in these genera, it is important that the garden pool be located in a sunlit area. Soft sunny banks and snags projecting over and from the water should be provided.

Breeding occurs in the water. Courtship varies by species and sub-species. The males of some forms have elongated claws and hover in the water in front of the female, caressing her face and anterior shell with trembling claws. The males of short-clawed forms pursue the female, nipping at the trailing edge of her shell. In both cases, when the female becomes quiescent, copulation occurs.

Nesting in well-drained areas, the female sliders and cooters may produce multiple clutches, depositing from as few as 2 to more than 20 eggs. Depending on temperature and nest humidity, incubation can vary from about two months to nearly three months. Incubation temperatures should be maintained between 82 and 87°F (28–30°C) (see comments on incubation temperatures, page 39).

Primitive Side-Necked Turtles

The side-necked turtles are named for their characteristic of turning their heads to the side and hiding the head in the crook between the neck and the foreleg. All species of this family, the Pelomedusidae, occur in the world's tropics. These species may be encountered in northern South America, sub-Saharan Africa, Madagascar, and certain of the Indian Ocean islands.

The many species are primarily aquatic, but individuals of some may occasionally be encountered well away from water sources. This is especially true during the rainy season. One genus, *Pelusios,* the African mud turtle, apparently burrows into the earth to estivate/hibernate through the dry season.

Some species may emerge from the water to bask, especially when young. Others may simply crawl into shallow water or float at the surface of deeper water, exposing most or part of their carapaces to the sun. Many species get quite large; some are among the largest of freshwater turtles. Two of the New World species are considered endangered species; the populations of others may be dwindling. The two endangered species, riverine species of the genus *Podocnemis*, were once among the most abundant of the world's turtles. However, the collecting of eggs and adults for food and capture of hatchlings for the pet industry have severely depleted the breeding populations of *P. expansa* and *P. unifilis*, resulting in the endangered status of the two.

With age, some members of this family (*Erymnochelys madagascarien-*sis of Madagascar and *Peltocephalus dumeriliana* of Amazonian South America) develop greatly enlarged heads. While the enlarged heads of other turtle species are often associated with a shellfish diet, it seems that these two pelomedusine species feed largely on palm nuts.

Only *Pelusios*, the African mud turtles, have hinged plastra; all other genera have rigid plastra. Containing 14 species, *Pelusios* is also the largest genus in this family.

African Mud Turtles

None among the many species of this genus is brightly colored, but all are immensely hardy creatures that seldom develop health problems in captivity. For this reason we strongly recommend small *Pelusios* sp. for beginning hobbyists. Of the many species contained in this genus, surprisingly few species are available to

African mud turtles are hardy and underappreciated by hobbyists. Pictured is the common Pelusios subniger.

This frightened African roofed turtle, Pelomedusa subrufa, *has assumed a defensive posture.*

the pet trade. As a matter of fact, only one, the East African black mud turtle, *P. subniger*, is regularly seen.

Although they are hardy, please note that African mud turtles of all species often are aggressive toward other turtle species (and occasionally toward fingers). Their jaws are strong and aggression can quickly cause injury to other turtles or pain to a finger. The tails and trailing feet of basking turtles are often targeted by African mud turtles.

P. subniger is a rather smoothly domed turtle species that may retain growth annuli well into adulthood. It has neither a vertebral keel nor posterior serrations. We have heard these turtles likened in appearance to a stone with a head! Actually, once they are acclimated they are fairly active and are reasonably strong swimmers.

Sadly, few hobbyists are working with and breeding this turtle species, thus most East African mud turtles

available in the pet trade are wild-collected imported specimens.

In the wild, this species inhabits all manner of water holes, as well as swamps, marshes, and slowly flowing waters. They attain about 8 inches (20 cm) in length, but most examples seen in the pet trade are in the 3.5 to 5-inch (8.8–12.7 cm) size range. Sexually mature males have a slight plastral concavity and a longer, thicker tail than the females.

African mud turtles of all species are primarily carnivorous and will eat a wide variety of natural and prepared foods.

African Roofed Turtle

The single species in the African genus *Pelomedusa* is *P. subrufa*. Besides occurring in suitable habitats over most of sub-Saharan Africa, *Pelomedusa* is known from the island of Madagascar.

As with *Pelusios*, few hobbyists work with this wonderfully hardy, quietly colored, moderately sized—commonly to 6 inches (15 cm), rarely to nearly double that—side-necked turtle. The roofed turtle is much like the African mud turtles in habits and habitats. Virtually all specimens available in the pet trade are wild-collected imports. There is no reason that it cannot be captive-bred. It seems only because imported specimens are readily available at moderate prices that roofed turtles have not gathered much of a fan club. It is thought that only a single clutch is produced annually by a given female, but that one nesting can produce from 10 to more than 40 eggs. Should you wish to attempt breeding the species, you will first, of course, need adult specimens of both sexes, and we would suggest a slight winter cooling as well as a reduced winter photoperiod.

The carapace of the roofed turtle is flattened dorsally and usually of some shade of brown. If the posterior marginals are at all serrate, they are only weakly so. The dorsal surface of the head and neck and the anterior surface of the limbs are about the same color as the carapace. The ventral and posterior surfaces of the head, neck, and legs are much lighter, cream to yellow, often with an olive tinge. The plastron has no hinge, a feature that immediately distinguishes the roofed turtle from the African mud turtles.

Yellow-Spotted Side-Necked Turtle

Despite the fact that this is now considered an endangered species, captive-bred and hatched babies of the yellow-spotted side-necked turtle, *Podocnemis unifilis*, are still occasionally available to hobbyists. Before deciding to purchase these, see the cautions (page 24) regarding trading in endangered wildlife.

As with many turtles, it is the babies of this species that are the prettiest and the most in demand.

From the 1950s until their listing in the Endangered Species Act in June 1970, hundreds of thousands of hatchlings of this species were imported annually for the pet trade of the United States. Additional thousands were sent to Europe. Hundreds of thousands more eggs were consumed by Amazonian peoples for whom the eggs were a common marketplace item, and the adult turtles were also trapped for food. Although the designation of endangered largely curtailed the exportation for the pet marketplace, adults and eggs are still openly available in the marketplaces of Iquitos (Amazonas), Peru, and, we are told by knowledgeable sources, in the markets of many other cities and countries as well.

Appearance: This is basically a gray turtle. The anterior surfaces of the limbs and the dorsal surface of the head are somewhat darker than the

Now considered an endangered species, only captive-hatched specimens of the Amazonian yellow-spotted side-necked turtle, Podocnemis unifilis, *are now available to hobbyists.*

carapace. The yellow spots from which the common name is derived are on the head. There are nine of them— one atop the snout; one on each side of the head below the snout spot; one beneath, one posterior to, and one above and behind each eye. The overall impression is of a little grease-painted clown-turtle. The specific name of "unifilis" refers to the single chin barbel borne by turtles of this species in the Orinoco drainage area (for the turtles of the Amazonian drainages, which have two barbels, the name is less appropriate). Adult females are known to attain more than a 25-inch (63.5 cm) carapace length. Males are seldom more than half that size. The males have a much longer and thicker tail than the females.

Breeding: Females are known to nest up to three times in a season, producing from 8 to 20 (occasionally more) eggs per nesting. Gravid females are known to wander far from the water to find suitable nesting areas.

Breeding success with this interesting turtle is now rather regularly accomplished by both zoological gardens and private hobbyists. It is the progeny from these successes that are now offered by specialty dealers and the breeders themselves. The hatchlings have an overall ground color of warm olive-gray to olive-tan or olive-brown.

Habits: The yellow-spotted side-necked turtle is primarily an herbivorous species. In captivity it will eat many aquatic plants as well as fruits and many kinds of dark greens (no spinach or iceberg lettuce, please). Romaine, escarole, collards, squash, apples, grapes, and the like are all readily accepted. Trout and catfish chows can be fed in moderation. A specialized process of sub-surface particulate feeding is indulged in by this and other juvenile members of the genus *Podocnemis*; the jaws are held open just below the surface, and expansion of the throat pulls in surface water and its contents. Jaw contraction forces out water. Feeds with high levels of animal protein may eventually be shown to be detrimental to the long-term health of this turtle species, just as excess animal protein has proven to be to other herbivorous reptiles.

Yellow-spotted side-necked turtles are essentially aquatic. Although the babies can be kept in rather small quarters, the large size of adults makes indoor maintenance difficult. This is a species best worked with by hobbyists in the deep South, where outside facilities can be provided for year-round maintenance. All of the *Podocnemis* species are cold-sensitive and require winter heating.

Chelids

Advanced Side-Necks and Snake-Necks

The chelid turtles (family Chelidae) fold their heads and necks sideways, in front of their forelimbs, much like primitive side-necks or pelomedusines. The separation of these two families is based on bone structure and the placement of the gular scute on the plastron. Chelids are found in South America, Australia, and New Guinea.

The Advanced Side-Necks

These are for the most part easily maintained but essentially aquatic, turtle species. Fewer than a half dozen species are generally available, but among those are the most spectacular in appearance of all turtles.

The Matamata, *Chelus fimbriatus*

There may be a few turtle or tortoise hobbyists who have not met the remarkable turtle known as the matamata, for it is no longer commonly seen in the pet trade.

Appearance: The matamata is a typical chelid in that it folds its neck to the side to conceal its head. The long, thick neck of the matamata is laterally flattened and fringed with filamentous appendages of skin. But it is the head of the matamata that usually provokes most interest. The head is broadly triangular, noticeably flattened, and the curved jaws form an apparent and perpetual smile. The nostrils extend forward in a doubly cylindrical snorkel. The eyes are small and easily overlooked. A pliable, flat flap of skin extends from each temporal area.

The precise function of the cutaneous fringes and flaps that adorn the sides of the neck and chin remains largely conjectural. However, it is these flaps and fringes that yield the scientific name of *Chelus fimbriatus*, literally, the fringed turtle.

The fringes may help conceal the turtle by interrupting the outline. They may also serve as lures, when waving in the water, to bring fish prey closer. But there's a far greater function than we currently understand; these projections are highly innervated, and probably play a major role in prey detection and identification.

Despite their not inconsiderable size, when in habitat even adults of this normally slow-moving turtle can be easily overlooked. The rough shell of the matamata permits copious growths of algae to take hold, effectively concealing the turtle as a "wait-and-ambush" predator. While lying quietly, it waits for passing or inquisitive fish to come within the reach of the long neck. Then, with a forward lunge, and a corresponding distension of the throat, the widely opened maw sucks in water, fish, and all near it. The water and other unwanted debris are expelled, and the piscine prey swallowed. This method of hunting is often referred to as the "gape-and-suck" technique. In comparison with those of most turtles, the jaws of the matamata are weak. Its prey is swallowed entire in a series of gulping motions.

Occasionally matas may take a more active role in food procurement. We have seen ours actively pursuing fish, and even seeming to herd them into a corner of the tank where the fish are more vulnerable and easily caught.

In overall appearance, the matamata, Chelus fimbriatus, *is surely one of the world's most unique turtles.*

The matamata is a denizen of the Amazon and Orinoco drainages in the South American countries of Bolivia, Peru, Ecuador, Colombia, and Brazil. It has also been found in Trinidad, but is thought to have been washed to that island by flood conditions on the mainland.

Matas of all sizes are entirely aquatic. They inhabit shallow water, or slow-moving or nonmoving water. All manner of backwaters, pools, oxbows, and lakes are favored. Despite its aquatic propensities, the matamata is, at best, a weak swimmer. Adults and young alike need water sufficiently shallow to allow them to merely extend their long necks upward and break the surface with their snorkellike nose. The neck length exceeds that of the vertebral column!

The record shell size for this remarkable turtle is just over 17 inches (43 cm). Most individuals are somewhat smaller. Females attain slightly greater sizes than the males. Males have a proportionately longer, heavier tail than the females.

Although no subspecies have been described, there appear to be a few rather constant geographical differences in both color and shell shape (when viewed from above) when the turtles of the Orinoco are compared with those of the Amazon.

These differences are especially noticeable in the juveniles. The juveniles of the Orinoco drainage have a tan-to-caramel-colored carapace, a dark marking on the central protuberance of each pleural scute, and a narrow, dark vertebral stripe. The dorsal surface of the broadly triangular head and thick neck are rather similarly colored, but have a dark-outlined, broad central area slightly darker in color. The throat and ventral surface of the neck are rose to strawberry. The axillae, ventral surfaces of the legs, and soles of the feet are paler rose. The plastron is light, often with pinkish overtones, and with a dark smudge at each lateral seam. When viewed from above, the sides of the carapace are nearly straight.

Although the Amazonian matas have the same markings, the ground color (especially of those from Peru) is a much darker brown. When viewed from above, the carapace is broadly oval, having convex sides.

The current availability of matas in the pet trade is sporadic at best. The few that are imported command high prices. Even those that are available, have not necessarily been legally procured. A great many hatchling matas arrive as undeclared stowaways in tropical fish shipments. Lately a fair number of adult matas have also been imported. Simply because their size makes it difficult to hide them from customs and wildlife inspectors, most of the adult matas are probably legally imported.

Habits: Matamatas are nonbasking species. They are easily kept in suitably sized aquariums that contain sufficient water for the turtles to move about easily, but that are sufficiently shallow so the matas do not need to swim to reach the surface to breathe. In captivity many matamatas are quite active. Unless firmly anchored, all cage furniture will be persistently and ruthlessly rearranged. Outside box filters should be used to help maintain water clarity and quality. Even with filtration it will be necessary to change most of the water weekly. A complete cleaning should be done monthly. Chlorines, chloramines, and other additives should be removed from the water.

It is simple to feed matas. Newly acquired specimens may insist on a live fish diet. Even this is not difficult. We merely keep a fair number of food fish in the tank at all times. When sufficient prey items are available, matamatas grow rapidly. As captives, they quickly become accustomed to accepting dead fish and fish parts. Periodically place a capsule of multivitamin/mineral supplement in a proffered food item. It has been suggested that certain compounds present in goldfish are detrimental to the health of fish-eating reptiles. Therefore we use goldfish as dietary items only sporadically, providing minnows and shiners instead.

Breeding: Although the breeding biology of wild matamatas has often been reported, the species has proven rather difficult (but far from impossible) to breed when captive. Up to 28 eggs have been reported from wild clutches. To date, not only have captive clutches numbered considerably fewer, but hatching success has been relatively poor. Although wild matas reportedly prefer mud banks over sandbars for nesting, captives have accepted flat expanses of sand for nesting and deposition.

Captive incubation durations of the nearly spherical, hard-shelled eggs have averaged about 215 days. With a diameter of about 1⅜ inches (3.5 cm), the eggs are slightly larger than Ping-Pong balls. Apparently, only a single clutch is produced annually.

The Twist-Necked Turtle

Although this seems a singularly poor common name, since it is used so widely by both hobbyists and professional herpetologists, it seems foolish to try to change it here. The appearance of this turtle is revealed when its scientific name is literally translated: the generic name *Platemys* means flat turtle, and the specific name *platycephala* means flat head. This highly aquatic, depressed species is widely distributed in the Caribbean and Amazon drainages of northern South America. There are two seldom defined subspecies. The subspecies *platycephala*, of the eastern part of the range, is the lighter in coloration, hence, in the eyes of the hobbyist, the prettiest. The subspecies *melanonota*, of the more westerly areas of the range, is the darker.

Appearance: *Platemys platycephala* is of moderate size, its bicarinate (two-keeled) carapace occasionally attaining a length of about 6.5 inches (16.5 cm). Most adults are an inch (2.5 cm) to a half an inch (1.3 cm) smaller. This is a

Dispersing during periods of flood, the tropical South American twist-necked turtle, Platemys platycephala melanonota, *is often left high and dry by receding waters.*

91

quietly colored but pretty species. The ground color is yellow-orange, terra-cotta, or dark brick red. Irregular, often rectangular or triangular patches of black pigment are usually present on the costal scutes and may involve the outer edges of the vertebrals as well. These markings are usually asymmet-ric. The vertebrals are longitudinally concave. The head is most often yel-lowish dorsally and black (or at least dark) laterally. Three dark stripes, two lateral and one dorsal, are present on the neck. Besides being flattened, the head is narrow and not greatly distinct in width from the neck. The black eyes are small but distinct. The large plastron is slightly upturned at the front.

Habits: Like the sympatric mata-mata, the twist-necked turtle is not a strong swimmer. It frequents heavily vegetated and shallow waters. Bill Lamar has mentioned encountering specimens wandering in the forest, well away from the closest water.

Breeding: Unusual for a turtle, this species seldom digs a nest. The single egg is deposited in moist leaf litter and haphazardly covered by the female. A frail attempt may be made to also scratch a little sand over the egg.

Since very few of these interesting and easily kept turtles have yet been captive-bred, those offered in the pet trade are wild-collected, imported specimens. Seemingly hatchlings and juveniles are less frequently found than adults, for small specimens are seldom offered for sale.

The diet of this turtle consists pri-marily of animal matter. Our speci-mens eat all manner of insects, pick snails from the water plants we period-ically gather and supply, and are par-ticularly fond of earthworms and small freshly killed fish, and Reptomin (pre-pared turtle food). Twist-necked turtles also reportedly eat some vegetation, but we have never seen ours doing so.

The Snake-Necks

The snake-necked turtles occur in southern South America, on the island continent of Australia, and in New Guinea. In all cases, the cervical vertebrae are longer than those of the trunk. In contrast to many of the short-necked members of this side-necked turtle family, the snake-necks are strong swimmers, and although com-mon in quiet lagoons, oxbows, and bill-abongs, they do not hesitate to enter deep and swiftly moving waters. The South American snake-necks have proven far more difficult to maintain in captivity than their Austro-Papuan relatives.

South American Snake-Necked Turtle

Of this bitypic genus, only one species, the South American side-necked turtle, *Hydromedusa tectifera*, is available in the pet marketplace, and then only from specialist dealers. Its congener, Maximilian's snake-neck, *H. maximiliani,* is poorly known, even to field researchers.

Not only is the South American snake-necked turtle the prettiest of the world's snake-necks, it has the dubi-ous distinction of being the most diffi-cult to successfully maintain as well. Pet marketplace needs are fulfilled with wild-collected imported speci-mens. Many of these arrive in the United States and Europe in weak-ened condition and some never eat voluntarily. Captive specimens also seem especially prone to bacterial problems that cause shell and mouth rot. Since we're not sure that there is such a thing as an entirely healthy imported South American snake-necked turtle, we will merely caution that it is important to begin by acquir-ing the healthiest-*looking* specimen possible. It is also important to have access to a qualified reptile veterinar-ian—just as a backup.

The Argentine snake-necked turtle, Hydromedusa tectifera, *is a coveted but difficult captive.*

After acquisition of specimens of which the health is not already threateningly compromised, good filtration and frequent water changes to prevent bacterial buildup are mandatory.

Appearance: Healthy examples of this turtle, kept in a large, clean, and properly appointed display can be quite spectacular. Even when resting on the bottom of their tank with neck fully extended, looking alertly around (as they often do), healthy specimens of this turtle are sure to catch the attention of passersby. The overall aspect is of a bright-eyed snake crawling out from beneath a rough gray rock.

H. tectifera attains a carapace length of about 12 inches (30 cm). Most of those seen in our pet trade are between 4 and 7 inches (10–17 cm) in shell length.

Conical projections, best defined on smaller turtles and largest posteriorly, appear on most of the costal and vertebral scutes. Concentric growth annuli can be quite distinct. The carapace is variably gray, the plastron yellow, with or without brown smudging or blotching. The head and neck is gray dorsally. A broad, black-bordered yellow stripe is present on the sides of the head, beginning at the snout and extending along the neck. The ventral surface of the head and neck is yellowish. The limbs are gray on their anterior surfaces and yellowish on the posterior surface.

Males have a discernible plastral concavity and a longer, thicker tail than the females.

Breeding: This snake-necked turtle has not been captive-bred more than a handful of times. The only nesting we have observed was that by a freshly imported 6.5-inch-long (16 cm) female. She dug a rather deep nest in the sand at the edge of her water receptacle and

The New Guinean Siebenrock's snake-necked turtle, Chelodina siebenrocki, is now being bred in captivity. A juvenile specimen is pictured here.

Australian and Papuan Snake-Necked Turtles

Although it has long been illegal to export any of Australia's herpetofauna for personal or commercial reasons, many of these laws have been circumvented by both European and American hobbyists. Because of these circumventions, several species of captive-bred and hatched Australian snake-necked turtles are now available to hobbyists on both continents. Even though originally of dubious legality, it seems that herpetoculturists now feel it is safe to traffic in the captive-bred and hatched offspring of these interesting creatures, for babies are now offered and traded freely in the pet marketplaces. The Papuan species are now being imported under permit and seem entirely legal.

The Austro-Papuan snake-necked turtles can be roughly divided into two species groups, the narrow-carapaced (such as *Chelodina oblonga* and *C. seibenrocki*) and the broad-carapaced (such as *C. longicollis* and *C. novaguineae*). Most seen in the pet trade of the United States are in the latter group.

Species from southern Australia are quite cold-tolerant; some even hibernate in the wild. Those from northern Australia and Papua/New Guinea are cold-sensitive and must be kept warm year-round. All species are persistently aquatic, but some specimens wander a fair distance from water. Despite the fact that most species prefer to eat under water, our Australian snake-necks would come to the side of their enclosure to accept small fish and pink mice, then swallow the tidbits on land. Although without the lubrication of the water it was a laborious procedure, some turtles accomplished the feat time and again.

Appearance: Except for *C. parkeri* of New Guinea, which has prominent light reticulations on its head, the

deposited 5 eggs. None developed. Winter cooling and a shortened photoperiod may be necessary to induce reproductive cycling.

Habits: These turtles catch small fish and tadpoles by using the "gape-and-suck" technique described in the account of the matamata (page 89). When eating aquatic insects or larger pieces of fish, this turtle merely grasps them in its jaws and positions the morsel with its forefeet. The turtle does this with its neck ess-shaped close to the carapace edge. Despite its rather weak jaws, this turtle is reputedly very fond of snails. The shells of small snails are summarily crushed and the entire thing swallowed. Larger snails are reportedly removed in some manner through the opercular opening, the shell remaining intact. We have not personally observed this.

Austro-Papuan snake-necks display no contrasting colors. The carapaces are olive-gray to black, the plastrons are usually light with dark pigment outlining each scute, limbs and dorsal surfaces of head and neck are pretty much the same color as the carapace, but the ventral surface of the neck and the chin are light (often yellowish). The comparative width of the forelobe of the plastron often figures prominently in species identification.

The Common Snake-Necked Turtle

Known scientifically as *C. longicollis*; this is the species of snake-necked turtle most often seen in American herpetoculture. These turtles occur in eastern Australia from tropical northern Queensland to temperate southern New South Wales and South Australia. The southernmost populations hibernate. This species has a smooth oval carapace that may be gently domed, somewhat flattened, or even have a weak to moderate longitudinal depression for the length of the carapace. The vertebral concavity may play an interesting role in reproduction in the populations that have it. Males overtaking the females seem to orient themselves by following the concave vertebral area with their chin. However, specimens that lack the central concavity seem to do equally well in reproducing. At its widest point, the forelobe of the plastron of *C. longicollis* is as wide as the marginal scales, or wider. Adults may attain a length of 10 inches (25 cm). Most are smaller. Some males of this species have noticeably concave plastra, others only weakly so. Males do have a much longer and thicker tail than the females.

In southwestern Florida, our common snake-necks were kept outside year-round. They were active even during the coolest weather, but on cold *and* overcast days they seldom left their pond (a 6-foot (1.8 m) diameter kiddie wading pool, sunk to its rim in the ground with a low fence a few feet away). On sunny days, whether temperatures were cold or not, the turtles would usually haul out and bask periodically.

That their lifestyle was oriented by *our* seasons and photoperiods (exactly reversed from those of Australia in the southern hemisphere) was attested by the fact that our snake-necks nested naturally each summer. Females would often nest as far from the "pond" as the confines of their enclosure would allow. The nests were about 5 inches (12.5 cm) deep and well able to accommodate the 5 to 12 eggs produced (some females are known to have produced up to two dozen eggs). With their long necks and rough shells, the babies are endearing creatures. They begin feeding as soon as the yolk sac is entirely absorbed and initially accept tiny (male guppy-sized) fish and chopped earthworms. The adults were fond of thawed frozen fish, worms, and trout and catfish chows. They would carefully comb through aquatic plants for snails and other organisms but did not seem to eat the plants themselves.

New Guinea Snake-Necked Turtle

Virtually everything said about *C. longicallis*, except for its tolerance for cold, applies equally to the rather similar New Guinea snake-necked turtle, *C. novaguineae*. The New Guinea snake-neck is a very tropical species that is usually browner than *C. longicollis*. Also, at its widest, the anterior plastral lobe of the New Guinea snake-neck is seldom wider than the inner seams of the marginal scutes. This species may also attain a 10-inch (25 cm) carapace length, but is usually two or three inches (5–8 cm) smaller.

Red-Bellied Short-Necked Turtle

This is the only member of this genus of five Australian and Papuan species

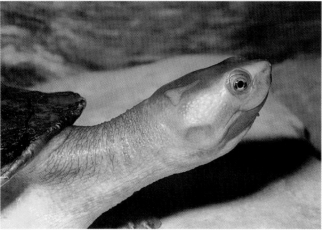

Compare the brilliance of the head markings of this hatchling New Guinean red-bellied short-necked turtle, Emydura subglobosa, *(top) with the faded pattern of the adult (bottom).*

yellow with growth. The carapace is smoothly domed, nonserrate, and some shade of brown in color.

Adults of this species offered for sale have usually been imported from New Guinea; hatchlings offered for sale are usually captive-bred and hatched. Many hobbyists, both in the United States and Europe, work successfully with this attractive turtle.

It seems that females attain sexual maturity at about 6.5 inches (16.5 cm) in carapace length. Males can be somewhat smaller. Clutches number from 3 (small young females) to 12 (large adult females) with from 5 to 7 being the norm. Females in our care nested at a distance of several feet (1 m) from their pond. Had they not been stopped by the confines of their enclosure, they might have gone even farther. Although they usually nested in fairly open areas, one female seemed to prefer to construct her nests at the base of Heliconia canes shading the enclosure. Head bobs and stroking of the female's head and neck by the male occur while the pair are swimming or hovering in the water. The nests averaged four inches (10 cm) in depth and easily accommodated all eggs. Our females did not take many pains to conceal the nest after egg deposition.

Hatchlings of this species were alert and wary. On the occasions when they were approached while sunning, they would scurry and tumble into the water. The adults would allow us quite near them before tumbling into the water if we approached the enclosure slowly. Once in the water, they apparently felt more secure, and would take pieces of fish from our fingers. Besides fish, *E. subglobosa* readily accept trout and catfish chows, dried cat chow, snails, small mussels, crickets, and earthworms. They are a tropical species that must not be allowed to cool significantly in winter.

that is commonly seen in captivity. Although its correct scientific name is *Emydura subglobosa*, this rather large—to 9 inches (22.8 cm)—and attractive side-necked turtle is often offered for sale as *E. albertisii.* Although it fades to yellow as adulthood is approached, the plastron of hatchlings and juveniles is a very bright pink to pinkish-red. Reddish-pink stripes also occur on the head and neck. Like the plastron, these stripes become more

The True Tortoises

Creatures of the Land

With but a single exception, the true tortoises (family Testudinidae) are moderately to highly domed terrestrial turtles ranging from small—2.5 inches (6 cm), to huge—more than 40 inches (100 cm). The single exception to the domed carapace is the curiously flattened pancake tortoise, *Malacochersus tornieri* of eastern Africa. Most tortoises live more than 25 years, many far longer than that.

Until the mid-1980s, tortoises were rather readily available and quite inexpensive. Today, with the exception of the African hinge-backed tortoises, genus *Kinixys*, (which are somewhat difficult to acclimate), this is no longer the case. Most tortoises are now protected by international law or regulation. Many once commonly seen species are no longer available, a few are sporadically so, and if exportation for the pet trade is allowed, it is usually on a quota system. The result of the curtailed importation has been higher prices and greater interest in captive-breeding projects.

It is important to consider several things when you purchase a tortoise. Among these is the space available (if you have only a 2 × 4 foot (.6 × 1.2 m) cage you should not purchase a spur-thighed tortoise, *Geochelone sulcata*, which may near 100 pounds (45 kg) in weight when it is adult). If you live in the humid Southeast you might wish to rethink your pending purchase of an arid-land tortoise, such as the Egyptian tortoise, *Testudo kleinmanni*.

Unless you have enough space for large tortoises, tailor your choice of specimens to conditions available. If you live in a humid area (or a fog belt) consider the red-footed or yellow-footed tortoise, *Geochelone carbonaria* or *G. denticulata*. For small indoor facilities buy small tortoise species. *Testudo hermanni*, the Herrmann's tortoise, is one of the better species; the elongated tortoise, *G. elongata*, is another. If you do have a fair expanse of yard that you can dedicate to a tortoise area and if you live in Florida, Texas's Rio Grande valley, or other nearly perpetually hot area, and if you enjoy larger tortoises, you have a lot of choices. A Leopard tortoise, *G. pardalis*, a spur-thighed tortoise, or even an Aldabra tortoise, *G. gigantea*, may be just the ticket. All are now captive-bred in fair numbers.

Tortoises are largely, but not exclusively, herbivorous. In the wild, many will consume carrion, insects, or even nestling rodents or birds if they happen across them. Captives of most species will eagerly eat dark leafy vegetables (romaine, escarole), pulpy fruit (such as squashes), fruits (apples, pears, kiwis, tomatoes) and a very little prepared tortoise diet or dog kibble. There are several tortoise diets now on the market that claim to offer complete nutrition, but we would still recommend variety. We know that the fruit/veggie diet works, for we've had some of our tortoises for more than 40 years. We periodically add a D_3-calcium supplement to the food.

Vitamin/mineral supplements are given to rapidly growing young tortoises more frequently than to adults. Many tortoises will breed year-round;

others (especially species from temperate areas or tropical areas having well-defined rainy and dry seasons) have one or two circumscribed breeding seasons annually. In most cases breeding will occur in the spring when the hours of daylight are increasing, or at the advent of the rainy seasons. Low barometric pressure (if accompanied by suitably warm temperatures) may stimulate breeding year-round.

Nesting is a lengthy process for the stub-toed tortoises. Depending on soil composition, it may take our radiated tortoises, *Geochelone radiata*, from two to four hours to complete the nesting sequence. (When we lived in North Carolina, where the soil was red clay, our female gave up on nesting after eight hours of attempted digging. We provided an alternate nesting site.) Gopher tortoises, *Gopherus polyphemus*, which have nested in our yard, take a shorter time for nest preparation, but they often dig their nests in the yielding sand aprons that front their burrows.

Egg incubation may be divided into two types; low humidity and high humidity (please see comments on incubation, page 39).

South American Tortoises

Despite its vast continental expanse, South America has comparatively few tortoises. The two that we continue to see with some degree of regularity are the red-footed and the yellow-footed tortoises. These two species do well in humid situations. The red-foot is both a savanna and forest-edge species, while the yellow-foot seems more restricted to forests.

The natural range of the red-footed tortoise is from Panama to Argentina (mostly east of the Andes) and some West Indian Islands. Within that range there is apparently much variation in adult size and color. You may see reference to "Paraguayan red-headed or cherry-headed" red-foots, or Paraguayan dwarfs (the same as the red-headed ones), or "Bolivian giants," or "Colombians" (these latter have prominently concave shell sides), or any of several other designations. The prices of some are higher than those of others, but none is inexpensive any longer.

Although many are smaller, red-foots often attain a foot (30 cm) in length and some near 18 inches (45 cm). The elongate shell is highly domed, of a dark ground color and, when viewed from above, has parallel

Once imported in large numbers for the pet trade, the availability of red-footed tortoises for the pet trade is now largely dependent on captive-breeding programs. The hatchlings (top) are quite different in appearance than the adults (bottom).

to concave sides. The anterior marginals, even of hatchlings, are nonserrate. There is a light yellow to orange spot in the center of each of the costal and vertebral scutes, and a less well-defined light spot often occurs on each marginal. The scales of the head and forelimbs may vary from yellow through orange to red. Typically, the scales of the forelimbs are brighter than those of the head.

Yellow-footed tortoises attain a much greater size than the rather closely allied red-foot. In bygone days some of the yellow-footed tortoises seen in the pet trade were close to 30 inches (76 cm) in shell length. Apparently they came from the forested tri-country area of Amazonian Colombia, Peru, and Brazil. Today, only seldom are wild-collected yellow-foots of any size available. Almost all specimens offered for sale are captive-bred hatchlings. Babies are round when viewed from above but elongate with maturity. The carapace color is yellowish, often with gray or brown overtones. The scales of the head and forelimbs are yellow. Anterior marginals are serrate.

Both the red-footed and yellow-footed tortoises are very hardy and pretty species that we strongly recommend as starter tortoises. Of course, there are many very advanced hobbyists who prize these species, too. We do urge that you acquire captive hatched babies whenever possible. Even the hatchlings are hardy and readily accept a variety of food. As the tortoises approach sexual maturity, you will note that males are often less highly domed and have a broader carapace than the females. Males also have concave plastra and a heavier, longer tail than females. Courtship involves a species-specific series of head bobs and nods as well a series of chuckling vocalizations. After immobilizing the female by nipping her shell and limbs, the male mounts and breeds her. Small to moderate clutches (3 to 10 eggs) are usually produced by adult females. In the "humid" incubator at 82–86°F (28–30°C), incubation varies from 100 to nearly 180 days.

African Tortoises

We will divide this discussion into four parts—the North African tortoises, *Testudo kleinmanni* and *T. graeca*; the "typical" African tortoises, *Geochelone sulcata* and *G. pardalis*; the hinge-backed tortoises of the genus *Kinixys;* and, lastly, the unique pancake tortoise, *Malacochersus tornieri*.

In this discussion we will encounter two very different tortoise species with the same common name. These are the two spur-thighed tortoises: 1) the small—rarely to 12 inches (30 cm), more commonly to 8 inches (20 cm)—*Testudo graeca* (once referred to as the "Greek tortoise"), which occurs in a small part of Europe, but ranges widely over much of southern Asia and Northern Africa; 2) the immense—to 30 inches (76 cm)—*Geochelone sulcata* from the southern edge of the Sahara Desert. This is a perfect example of why it is better to learn and use scientific names of reptiles and amphibians.

Although not as commonly seen in the pet trade today as in past years, *T. graeca* ssp. is still one of the more commonly encountered forms. Pet trade trafficking is probably directly responsible for severely depleting populations of this turtle in many areas of its range. Fortunately, despite wild-collected adults still being the most commonly seen and inexpensive, a number of hobbyists are now breeding the several difficult-to-identify subspecies of this little tortoise.

T. graeca can be difficult to acclimate to captive conditions, especially in perpetually humid areas. When maintenance is attempted in such areas, respiratory ailments are not uncommon. Despite treatment, these often worsen

The East African pancake or soft-shelled tortoise, Malacochersus tornieri, *is one of the most unusual and divergent of the true tortoises.*

color is tan to horn and patches of dark pigment usually are present. In some populations the dark coloration predominates. The head is dark, the limbs light, and a projecting conical tubercle, the "spur" from which the common name is derived, is present on each side of the tail.

Breeding: The techniques needed to cycle this tortoise for breeding will vary. In some cases, considerable winter cooling may be necessary but, in the case of tortoises from nonhibernating populations, hibernating the tortoise may do far more harm than good. Breeding, an affair where the male butts, shoves, and bites the female, occurs in the spring of the year. Nesting occurs several weeks later. From one to a dozen eggs are laid. Some females dig well-formed, substantial nests; others (at least in captivity) may do little more than dig a shallow depression and place a dusting of earth over the eggs laid therein. Some females may produce more than a single egg clutch in a season.

In appearance the little Libyan and Egyptian tortoise, *T. kleinmanni,* is much like a dwarfed, somewhat more highly domed and proportionately more elongate *T. graeca.* This species has only recently become available in the pet industry, and it seems unlikely that populations can sustain the present level of collecting without rapidly diminishing in numbers. The Egyptian tortoise is an arid-land species of brushy and sparsely vegetated habitats. It is adult at only 5 inches (12.7 cm) in length. Because of its newness in the pet trade, we are only now learning the techniques necessary to successfully keep and breed this little tortoise. It requires low humidity as well as moderate daytime temperatures. The Egyptian tortoise has been bred only a handful of times. That with proper preparation it can be both kept and bred successfully in adverse climates, is attested by the

or reoccur and can be fatal. It is somewhat easier to succeed with this tortoise species in dry-to-arid regions.

To do best with this species, it is necessary to know where your specimen originated. In some areas of its range this tortoise hibernates (brumates) in winter and estivates in excessively hot summer weather. In other areas it may do one or the other, and specimens in yet other populations remain active year-around.

The most successful breeders of the various *Testudo* species advocate an entirely herbivorous diet.

T. graeca may be found from seashore dunes to rocky mountain steppes at considerable elevations. It is most often associated with sparsely vegetated, dry areas but may occasionally wander temporarily into damper areas. Typically, these tortoises are most active in the morning.

While they are certainly not brightly colored, spur-thighed tortoises are variable and attractive. The ground success of the Tortoise Trust of the United Kingdom. Andy Highfield, Director of the Trust, has found that when a daytime temperature of much above 84°F (29°C) is provided, the tortoises become relatively inactive and attempt to estivate (as they would at excessively high temperatures in the wild). Highfield provides temperatures ranging from 62 to 82°F (16.6–28°C). His tortoises are most active when they are well illuminated and at temperatures in the 72 to 78°F (22–25.5°C) range. The minimum size of the caging he suggests is 2×5 feet (.6 $\times$ 1.5 m) and each cage can be expanded to twice that length. The retaining wall need not exceed 6 inches (15 cm). The Tortoise Trust uses a dry loam/sand substrate for these and other small arid-land tortoises.

The courtship of the Egyptian tortoise is gentler than that of many other chelonians. Head bobbing and butting are commonplace signs, but there seems to be a minimum of the biting and nipping indulged in by many other tortoise species.

Despite the preference of the tortoises for moderate temperatures, the Tortoise Trust has found that the eggs incubate most successfully at somewhat higher than usual temperatures. Highfield advocates a temperature of about 91°F (32.7°C) with a slight rise in temperature during the second trimester. Under this regimen the eggs hatch after about two months of incubation.

The most commonly seen of the two subspecies of leopard tortoises is the highly domed *Geochelone pardalis babcocki*, the race that occurs over much of southern Africa (except for the southwestern section). Although some specimens may attain slightly more than a 2-foot (61 cm) shell length, most are much smaller. Females of 1 foot (30 cm) in length are known to produce viable eggs that have been

The various forms of the Mediterranean spur-thighed tortoise, Testudo graeca *ssp., continue to be the most readily available of the European and North African tortoises.*

fertilized by males several inches (8 cm) smaller. Multiple clutches are usually produced by each sexually active female. These are laid at three- to four-week intervals and may number from 4

Although still imported from southern Africa in small numbers, most leopard tortoises available to hobbyists are now captive-bred. Compare the pattern of this hatchling Geochelone pardalis babcocki *with that of the adult on page 29.*

does have a weak plastral concavity (not present in females) and the tail is somewhat longer and heavier than that of the female.

The natural habitat of the leopard tortoise is variable (open woodlands, scrub, grasslands, and savannas) but always in rather arid, well-drained areas. Some specimens rather readily adapt to humid conditions (the south-eastern United States or isolated fog belts elsewhere) but many will require lengthy acclimatization. We have found that this species seems rather susceptible to respiratory problems when it is maintained in humid areas, especially when temperatures cool. However, once acclimatized, and if otherwise properly cared for, these tortoises will live for several decades in captivity. Because of their large adult size, leopard tortoises are best maintained outside whenever possible.

In coloration leopard tortoises may vary from sparsely to heavily patterned. The namesake leopard spots are present only on juvenile specimens. These fragment with advancing age and other more irregular markings may form. The edges of each scute are usually the lightest in color. The ground color is tan, yellow, or (when adult) some shade of dusty brown. The smudges are black.

Although its unmarked tan to brown coloration (often darker on scute edges) makes the big—20 to 30-inch (50–75 cm) long—African spur-thighed tortoise, *G. sulcata*, anything but showy, this species is hardy, adaptable, and personable. The sexes are rather difficult to identify, but females are smaller than males, have the smaller tail, and do not have the weak plastral concavity of most males.

Hatchlings have somewhat brighter hues than adults, but by comparison only. When properly cared for, hatchlings grow very rapidly. They reach large sizes and sexual maturity in just

Neither the adults (top) nor the hatchlings (bottom) of the sub-Saharan spur-thighed tortoise, Geochelone sulcata, *are brilliantly colored. This largest of the world's mainland tortoises is now captive-bred in considerable numbers.*

to 14 (by small females) to more than 30 (by larger females) in each clutch. They incubate easily in a low humidity incubator, hatching in about three months at 86°F (30°C). Hatchlings are beautifully and contrastingly colored in light yellow and black. Sexual differences are rather slight. The adult male a few years. When you are considering the purchase of babies, their adult size and the caging space required by adults should be kept in mind.

As mentioned earlier, the range of this, the largest of the world's mainland tortoises, runs roughly along the southern edge of the Sahara Desert. Thus, in nature it is an arid-land species. Additionally, it is an accomplished burrower. I have had specimens that have dug burrows 4 feet (1.2 m) deep and more than 20 feet (6 m) long. Other specimens, though, have merely pushed their way beneath shrubs and made shallow pallets to which they regularly retreated.

Sulcata breed readily in captivity. Like the leopard tortoise, female *G. sulcata* dig well-formed, deep nesting holes. The clutch size varies from 5 to about 18 eggs, but 7 to 10 seems most common. Females often dig well down into the soil with their forefeet before reversing position and digging the actual nesting chamber with their rear feet. At temperatures of 83 to 86°F (28–30°C) incubation lasts for about three months. In nature, incubation durations of up to seven months have been reported.

Both the leopard and spur-thighed tortoises are preferentially vegetarians. Wild specimens eat many types of grasses, succulents, and fungi. Captives eat many kinds of available greens, pulpy vegetables, and fruits. A very little dog chow can also be offered. Excesses of animal protein in the diet have now been linked to reptilian gout and abnormal carapacial growth (pyramiding). The carapaces of both species normally retain prominent growth rings.

The hinge-backed tortoises are all members of the genus *Kinixys*. Perhaps because Kinixys are readily available and are delicate and often difficult to acclimate, the prices of most species of this genus remain low.

Four species of hinge-backed tortoises are still imported in some numbers. All are shy and difficult to acclimate. Pictured is the Home's hinge-back, Kinixys homeana.

The available species vary in habitat preference, from rather dry (*K. b. belliana* & *K. (b.) spekii*), through moderately wet (*K. homeana),* to damp or wet (*K. erosa*). Sadly, most *Kinixys* that arrive in the pet trade of the United States are severely stressed (starved, desiccated, and parasitized) and succumb, even with qualified veterinary intervention, within a few months.

Although we strongly urge against the purchase of these tortoises, the inexpensive price entices many buyers. If you do purchase a hinge-backed tortoise, we urge you to have fecal floats and the necessary deparasitizing performed *immediately* by a qualified reptile veterinarian.

The several species of *Kinixys* are more omnivorous than many other tortoise species. Besides grasses and other greens, pulpy vegetables, and fruits, these tortoises eat slugs, snails, worms, and other invertebrates and carrion. Specimens kept at the Chicago Zoological Park (Brookfield Zoo) chased down and consumed young mice.

Unlike any other tortoises, all species in this genus have a hinge that allows downward motion in the posterior portion of the domed, elongate carapace. Thus, the posterior portion of their carapace can be closed downward against the rear of the plastron to afford protection to the legs and tail. All species are of moderate size—5 to 10 inches (12.5–25 cm), with *K. erosa* being the largest.

K. belliana is often referred to as "Bell's hinge-back." It is a species of brushy savanna and grassland, often encountered near waterholes. Well-defined wet/dry seasons predominate within the range of this species, and the tortoises often estivate when water sources are dried. *K. erosa* and *K. homeana* are known respectively as the serrated and the Home's hinge-backs. They are both rain forest species that are associated with marsh, swamp, and lake edges. Since both have strongly flaring anterior marginals, their identifications are confused by both dealers and hobbyists. Even adults of the serrated hinge-backed tortoise have strongly serrate, but not strongly flaring posterior marginals, while adults of the Home's hinge-back are not strongly serrate but do flare widely. The juveniles of both species have serrate marginal scales. Both the serrated and the Home's hinge-backed tortoise should be given a shallow water dish with easy access and egress and enough room to sit and soak.

Of the three species mentioned here, only Bell's hinge-back basks extensively. The perpetually warm and humid habitats of the other two enables them to remain suitably warm without basking.

Juveniles of all three species are more colorful than adults. *K. belliana* is variably marked and may have rather easily visible carapacial radiations. *K. erosa* may have yellowish or cream spotting and may or may not have a wide band of cream color at the base of the costal scutes. If *K. homeana* has any contrasting markings, they are usually only weakly defined.

The males of all hinge-backs have longer and heavier tails than the females, and a plastral concavity is also present. Adults of these are not difficult tortoises to sex. Despite this, few hinge-backs of any species have survived in captivity long enough to have been bred. It is known that clutches are small (from 1 to 4 eggs) and that incubation in the wild may take as long as five months. Incubation would probably be of much shorter duration under ideal captive conditions.

The most remarkable of the world's tortoises is the little East African pancake or soft-shelled tortoise, *Malacochersus tornieri*. This is a flattened tortoise that is adult at only 4.5 to 6 inches (11.4–15.2 cm) in length. The carapace is of some shade of tan or brown, and radiating markings of variable intensity may or may not be present. A single egg is produced at each nesting, but several nestings occur annually. With such a low reproductive rate, the onslaught of collecting for the pet trade has severely depleted the populations of this tortoise in many areas of its range. It has now been bred in captivity. Incubation takes several months in a low-humidity incubator at 84 to 86°F (28.8–30°C). Hatchlings are proportionately much more highly domed than the adults.

This little vegetarian is a hardy species and if provided with dry warm quarters is easily kept. It will eat grasses and both leafy and pulpy vegetables in captivity. Augmentation of this diet with some fruit is acceptable.

In natural habitat, the pancake tortoise is an agile denizen of arid, rock-strewn savannas. (Yes! A tortoise can be agile!) The pliable shell allows the tortoise to avoid predators by entering narrow fissures where it then holds itself in place with its strongly clawed limbs. It is now known that the pancake tortoise does not wedge itself in place by inflating its lungs and expanding its height, as once thought.

Asian Tortoises

Although there are many species of tortoises indigenous to Asia, few are now available in the pet trade. We will discuss only two species, the star tortoise, *Geochelone elegans*, and the elongated tortoise, *G. elongata*.

The 6 to 11-inch-long (15–28 cm) star tortoise is now captive-bred in fair numbers. This is fortunate, for it is one of the most beautiful of the world's tortoise species. Its black shell is elongate, highly domed, and vividly marked on each scute with a series of bright yellow radiations. It is indigenous to India, Sri Lanka, and Pakistan and is associated with relatively humid forested areas. It either forages early in the day or is quiescent during dry periods, but it may wander, feed, and breed throughout the daylight hours during the rains and monsoons. The largest specimens are found in Sri Lanka.

Males of this beautiful tortoise are very aggressive, both toward other males and toward females during breeding attempts. Considerable ramming, butting, and biting is indulged in. Wheezing chuckles are voiced by breeding males.

Star tortoises dig deep, flasked nests in which from 2 to 10 (usually 4 to 6) eggs are placed. In a humid incubator, at 84 to 86°F (28.8–30°C), incubation lasts from 85 to 95 days. Natural incubation may be nearly two months longer. The babies are vividly marked, but not as intricately as the adults.

In direct contrast to the star tortoise, the similarly sized elongated tortoise has a ground color of horn and may or may not be smudged with black. It is not a colorful species, but it is alert,

The hatchlings (top) of the infrequently available and expensive star tortoise, Geochelone elegans, *are less busily patterned than the adults (bottom). These specimens are of the large Sri Lankan form.*

hardy, and rather regularly available. It is interesting that the skin of the nose and around the eyes becomes suffused with rose-red during the breeding season. This seems brightest on male specimens. The carapace is highly domed, but is somewhat flattened dorsally. Elongated tortoises are now captive-bred in small numbers.

This, too, is an aggressive breeder. Some males have been so persistently aggressive toward the females that we have had to separate the two time and again. The nest of this species is small, at times being barely large enough to fully accommodate the 2 to 4 eggs. At 86°F (30°C) elongated tortoise eggs hatch after about 100 days of incubation.

This is another forest species that is fond of high humidity. It is found from India and surrounding countries to Vietnam and Malaysia.

American Tortoises

There are three species of true tortoises indigenous to the United States. All are in the genus *Gopherus*. All are protected either by state law (Texas tortoise, *G. berlandieri*) or both state and federal laws (gopher, *G. polyphemus*, and desert, *G. agassizii* tortoises). Permits are necessary before any of these can be legally collected or kept. In comparison with other tortoise species, our three native ones can be difficult to acclimate (especially if removed from natural habitat conditions) and all should be considered basically outdoor species. Both the gopher and the desert tortoise excavate extensive burrows. The Texas tortoise usually just plows shallow pallets into the earth beneath or against a shrub or clump of cacti. All three species are primarily vegetarian. Much of their food in the wild consists of harsh grasses and other similar vegetation. Morning glories, succulents, fruit and blossoms also figure prominently in the diet of all. The adult size ranges from 6 inches (15 cm) (Texas tortoise) to more than 12 inches (30 cm) (gopher and desert tortoises). All are brown to black when adult but more colorful as hatchlings. Growth annuli are usually retained by all three species throughout their long lives.

Of the three, the desert tortoises are most frequently seen. They have lived for more than five decades in captivity.

Contact the Game and Fish Commissions in your individual states for permit information.

European Tortoises

Finally, we introduce the most commonly seen European tortoise, the Hermann's, *Testudo hermanni* ssp. This small—to 7 inches (17.7 cm)—attractive tortoise ranges widely in suitably dry habitats on both the southern European mainland and on many of the adjacent islands. It favors open woodlands and scrub and dry areas overgrown by grasses and herbaceous plants. The carapace of *T. hermanni* is highly domed and hued in a ground color of horn. Black markings, variable in size, shape, and quantity are usually present. The posterior lobe of the plastron is weakly hinged. Hermann's tortoise has long been a favored pet species of cheloniophiles of the world. It is primarily a vegetarian, eating the typical tortoise fare of dark leafy vegetables, pulpy vegetables (such as squash), broccoli stems and leaves, flowers, and some fruit. This tortoise particularly favors clovers, dandelions and buttercups. Some specimens will prey on insects and other invertebrates as well as their more usual herbs and grasses.

Hermann's tortoise has been bred by both European and American hobbyists for many decades. Brumation is probably necessary for the long-term physiological well-being and breeding of this species. Males breed the females aggressively, butting and biting to immobilize their mates. Nests are flasked and about 4 inches (10 cm) deep. Several clutches of from 2 to 10 (occasionally more) eggs are laid annually by adult females. At from 83 to 86°F (28.3–30°C) incubation takes from 80 to 100 days. The hatchlings are hardy and grow quickly. It is suggested that minimal animal matter be fed the hatchlings of this tortoise species.

Soft-Shelled Turtles

Animated Flapjacks

Although they are every bit as recognizable as turtles as their hard-shelled relatives, the soft-shells, flattened and agile, are very different in many respects from the "typical" turtles.

The soft-shelled turtles are classified in the family Trionychidae. They are of North American, African, Asiatic, and East Indian distribution. Although hatchlings and young of some Asiatic species are occasionally available in the pet trade, most of those seen are North American spiny soft-shells, smooth soft-shells, and Florida soft-shells.

The carapace length of the adults of some Asiatic soft-shells exceeds a yard (1 m)—in the case of the gigantic Asiatic, *Pelochelys bibroni*, more than 4 feet (1.2 m) in length. The largest North American species is the Florida soft-shell, adult females of which attain a carapace length of just over 2 feet (.6 m); the largest recorded male is just half that size.

Habits: Although strong swimmers entirely at home in deep water, shallow river and lake edges are favored habitats. In these areas soft-shells will bury their shells into sand or mud and sit with only their necks and heads exposed. They like water sufficiently shallow so when the long neck is extended to the surface, they can breath without uncovering themselves.

Appearance: The carapace of the soft-shelled turtles is covered with a tough leathery skin. The carapace, rounded or oval when viewed from above, may bear a series of points (spines) along the front edge. American soft-shells that bear these projections are called the spiny soft-shells; those without spines are the smooth soft-shells. The forward edge of the carapace is flexible.

The neck is very long and fully retractile, the head is elongate and in most cases terminates in a long, flexible snout. The feet are broad, the toes fully webbed, and a flange of skin extends along the top edge of each forelimb. The soft-shell turtle is ever ready to use its claws and jaws, especially when handheld.

Soft-shelled turtles are often the colors of the mud or sand bottoms where they are found. Babies of some species may have pretty and prominent carapacial spots, which may be retained by the males, but are usually mostly or entirely obscured on the females.

The pallid soft-shelled turtle, Trionyx spinifer pallida, *occurs in eastern Texas and the contiguous areas of Oklahoma, Louisiana, and Arkansas.*

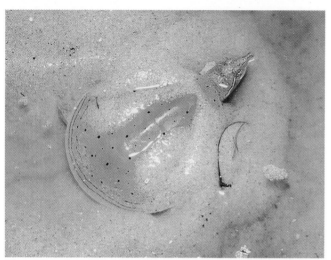

Like all members of the genus, the Gulf Coast spiny soft-shelled turtle, Trionyx spinifer aspera, *conceals itself in river bottom sand.*

With the exception of hatchling Florida soft-shelled turtles, *Trionyx ferox*, the members of this genus are easily maintained in captivity. Even the Florida species is easily kept once it has attained about 3.5 inches (9 cm) in length. Speculation continues regarding the frequent skin problems of captive hatchling Florida soft-shelled turtles. Although they occur in the wild in both clear and murky ponds and lakes, in waters having a wide range of acidity and alkalinity (pH), and in both fresh and weakly brackish habitats, baby Florida soft-shells are *extremely* prone to bacterial and fungal skin disorders that are difficult to reverse and invariably lethal if *not* reversed. We have had identical episodes with captive-hatched babies and with babies taken from the wild.

If of fungal origin, the problem may respond to a solution of acriflavine (follow directions of the package) or Betadyne in the water. Bacterial causes, of course, require a bactericide; since not all bacteria respond to the same medications, to effect a cure,

veterinary diagnosis and intervention is often required. As often as not, both fungal and bacterial agents attack together, further complicating treatment.

The problem of skin lesions developing on captive aquatic snakes was at least partially addressed several decades ago by herpetologist/showman, the late E. Ross Allen. While trying to maintain some of the difficult species, Allen began acidifying their aquarium water by adding freshly brewed tea in varying amounts. When combined with warmth—80 to 90°F (26.6–32.2°C)—skin lesions cleared. We have used this same concoction with hatchling Florida soft-shelled turtles with what seems some benefit. We would suggest that you experiment with water acidification if you intend to maintain hatchling Florida soft-shells. Six teabags placed for a few minutes in a small amount of boiling water, then added to 3 or 4 gallons (11.3–15.1 L) of aquarium water would be a starting point from which to weaken or strengthen the solution.

Baby soft-shells may be maintained in a fully aquatic setup with a substrate of water-*smoothed* river rock or clean *smooth* sand (sharp silica is apt to abrade the turtle's shell, giving fungal and bacterial problems an additional surface to invade). The soft-shell will probably bury itself in the sand but be unable to do so in the rock. Unless a *smooth* platform (of Styrofoam, corkbark, or plastic) is wedged at the surface so the turtle can emerge if it chooses, the water should be shallow enough for the turtle to reach the surface for breathing without swimming. The water should be clean, filtered, and partially changed weekly (or more often if it becomes fouled).

Soft-shells eat all manner of aquatic animal life in the wild and should be given worms (chopped if necessary), insects, and small fish (goldfish are not as good as shiners and minnows).

Some prepared foods are acceptable to some soft-shells.

The Florida soft-shelled turtle, *Trionyx ferox*, is more oval than the smooth or the spiny soft-shell. The babies are pretty little things, but can be difficult to maintain. The carapace is dark olive-green or olive-brown with darker oval ocelli. The carapace is rimmed with yellow posteriorly. This often shades to orange anteriorly. The dark head, neck, and limbs are spotted with yellow or orange. The plastron is gray anteriorly and charcoal posteriorly. This species has hemispherical projections on both the leading edge and anterior surface of the carapace.

The Gulf Coast spiny soft-shell, *T. spinifera aspera*, and the midland smooth soft-shell, *T. m. mutica,* are also often seen in the pet trade. These two forms are much easier to maintain successfully in captivity than the Florida species. Both have carapaces of olive-tan. That of the smooth soft-shell is often more richly colored but has only indistinct dark markings. The dark underside of the carapace contrasts strongly in color with the light plastron. On the other hand, the underside of the carapace of the spiny soft-shelled turtle is nearly as light in color as the plastron. Spiny soft-shells (there are actually six rather similar subspecies) have many small dark spots and ocelli on the carapace and streaks that coalesce into either one or two dark lines on the top rear of the carapaces. Males tend to retain the markings, but they obscure on the females with age and growth. Adult females of the smooth and spiny soft-shells are between 12 and 17 inches (30–43 cm) in length. Adult males may be only one-third the size of the females.

Caution: First, while baby soft-shells are harmless, larger specimens can and will bite and scratch painfully. Handle them with care! Second, *all* cage furniture provided soft-shells—ornaments, substrate, basking platforms—must be nonabrasive.

A Mention of Sea Turtles

It is quite likely that everyone in the world recognizes sea turtles. In the United States, a great amount of publicity is directed each summer toward the success (or lack of it) of these great paddle-limbed marine reptiles' nestings and hatchings.

Many persons find the hatchlings endearing creatures and occasionally try to maintain one or two in home aquariums. All species are considered either threatened or endangered. Unless you are a permitted research facility, the disturbing or keeping of the eggs or hatchlings of marine turtles is a legal offense. The best and only advice we will offer is "do not disturb!"

The black-knobbed, Graptemys n. nigrinoda, *is the only of the sawbacked map turtles that can be legally collected.*

At adulthood, this hatchling elongated tortoise, Geochelone elongata, *will measure nearly a foot in length.*

As it grows, the colors of this hatchling eastern painted turtle, Chrysemys p. picta, *will intensify.*

The yellow mud turtle, Kinosternon f. flavescens, *is widely distributed in the southcentral United States and adjacent Mexico.*

The pattern of yellow radiations against a background of black is typical of the European pond turtle, Emys orbicularis.

111

Useful Addresses and Literature

Turtle and Tortoise Clubs

There are several turtle and tortoise clubs in major cities in North America and Europe. Additionally, there are trusts dedicated to the conservation and preservation of the world's chelonians. Among the members and trustees are amateur enthusiasts and professional cheloniophiles. Most of the organizations produce informative newsletters and actively try to promote chelonian conservation and "chelonio-culture." All welcome inquiries and new members.

The Tortoise Trust
  BM Tortoise
  London WC1N 3XX
  England

California Turtle and Tortoise
  Club
  P.O. Box 7300
  Van Nuys, CA 91409

San Diego Turtle and Tortoise
  Society
  P.O. Box 519
  Imperial Beach, CA 91933

The New York Turtle and
  Tortoise Society
  163 Amsterdam Avenue, Suite 465
  New York, NY 10023

National Tortoise and Turtle
  Society
  P.O. Box 66935
  Phoenix, AZ 85082

SOPTOM
  Village des Tortues
  B.P. 24
  3590 Gonfaron
  France

Desert Tortoise Preserve
  Committee
  P.O. Box 453
  Ridgecrest, CA 93555

Society for the Study of
  Amphibians and Reptiles
  Dept. of Zoology
  Miami University
  Oxford, OH 45056

Gopher Tortoise Council
  c/o C. Small
  Department of Biology
  University of Central Florida
  4000 Central Park Boulevard
  Orlando, FL 32816

Herpetologist's League
  c/o Texas National Heritage
    Program
  Texas Parks and Wildlife
    Department
  4200 Smith School Road
  Austin, TX 78744

Fellow amateurs and professionals may also be found at the biology departments of museums, universities, high schools, and nature centers.

Books

Bartlett, Richard D. *In Search of Reptiles and Amphibians.* Leiden: E. J. Brill, 1988.

————. *Digest for the Successful Terrarium.* Morris Plains, NJ: TetraPress, 1989.

Conant, Roger & Joseph T. Collins. *Reptiles and Amphibians, Eastern/Central North America.* Boston: Houghton Mifflin, 1991.

Ernst, Carl H. et al. *Turtles of the United States and Canada.* Washington, DC: Smithsonian Inst. Press, 1994.

————. & R. W. Barbour. *Turtles of the World.* Washington, DC: Smithsonian Inst. Press, 1989.

Highfield, A. C. *Tortoise Trust Guide to Tortoises and Turtles.* 2nd ed., London: Carapace Press, 1994.

Stebbins, Robert C. *A Field Guide to Western Reptiles and Amphibians.* Boston: Houghton Mifflin, 1985.

Wilke, Hartmut. *Turtles, A Complete Pet Owner's Guide.* Hauppauge, NY: Barron's Educational Series, Inc., 1983.

This "business end" shot of an adult eastern snapping turtle, Chelydra s. serpentina, *clearly shows the massive build and outline of the formidable jaws.*

Hobbyist Magazines

Reptiles
P.O. Box 6050
Mission Viejo, CA 92690

The Reptilian Magazine
22 Firs Close
Hazlemere
High Wycombe
Bucks HP15 7TF
England

Reptile and Amphibian Magazine
RD3, Box 3709-A
Pottsville, PA 17901

Glossary

Albino Lacking black pigment.

Alveolar ridge (or plate) A broad crushing plate posterior to the mandibles.

Ambient temperature The temperature of the surrounding environment.

Anterior Toward the front.

Anus The external opening of the cloaca; the vent.

Bridge The "bridge of shell" between forelimbs and rear limbs that connects the carapace and the plastron.

Brumation The reptilian and amphibian equivalent of mammalian hibernation.

Carapace The upper shell of a chelonian.

Caudal Pertaining to the tail.

cb/cb Captive-bred, captive-born.

cb/ch Captive-bred, captive-hatched.

Chelonian A turtle or tortoise.

Chorioallantois The gas-permeable membranous layer inside the shell of a reptile egg.

Circadian rhythm Twenty-four hour cycle of biological activity.

Cloaca The common chamber into which digestive, urinary, and reproductive systems empty and which itself opens exteriorly through the vent or anus.

Congener A member of the same genus.

Crepuscular Active at dusk and/or dawn.

Debridement Surgical removal of diseased tissue.

Deposition As used here, the laying of the eggs or birthing of young.

Deposition site The nesting site.

Dimorphic A difference in form, build, or coloration involving the same species; often sex-linked.

Diurnal Active in the daytime.

Dorsal Pertaining to the back; upper surface.

Dorsum The upper surface.

Ecological niche The precise habitat utilized by a species.

Ectothermic Cold-blooded; lacking internal body temperature regulation.

Endemic Confined to a specific region.

Endothermic Warm-blooded.

Erythristic Having a prevailing red pigment.

Estivation A period of warm weather inactivity, often triggered by excessive heat or drought.

Form An identifiable species or subspecies.

Genus A taxonomic classification of a group of species having similar characteristics. The genus falls between the next broader designation of "family" and the next narrower designation of "species." *Genera* is the plural of *genus*. The genus is always capitalized.

Glottis The opening of the windpipe.

Gravid The reptilian equivalent of mammalian pregnancy.

Gular Pertaining to the throat.

Heliothermic Pertaining to a species that basks in the sun to thermoregulate.

Herpetoculture The captive breeding of reptiles and amphibians.

Herpetoculturist One who engages in herpetoculture.

Herpetologist One who engages in herpetology.

Herpetology The study (often scientifically oriented) of reptiles and amphibians.

Hibernaculum (pl. hibernacula) A winter den.

Hibernation Winter dormancy.

Hybrid Offspring resulting from the breeding of two species.

Hydrate To restore body moisture by drinking or absorption.

Immaculate Without colored spots.

Intergrade Offspring resulting from the breeding of two subspecies.

Juvenile A young or immature specimen.

Keel A carapacial or plastral ridge.

Lateral Pertaining to the side.

Mandibles Jaws.

Mandibular Pertaining to the jaws.

Melanism A profusion of black pigment.

Middorsal Pertaining to the middle of the back.

Monotypic Containing but one type.

Nocturnal Active at night.

Ocellus (pl. ocelli) An eyespot or eye-like colored spot.

Ontogenetic Maturation-related (color) changes.

Oviparous Reproducing by means of eggs that hatch after laying.

Pathogen A specific disease-causing agent.

Photoperiod The daily/seasonally variable length of the hours of daylight.

Plastron The bottom shell.

Poikilothermic (also ectothermic) A species with no internal body temperature regulation. The old term was "cold-blooded."

Postocular To the rear of the eye.

Race A subspecies.

Saxicolous Rock-dwelling.

Scute Scale.

Species A group of similar creatures that produce viable young when breeding. The taxonomic designation narrower than genus and broader than subspecies. Abbreviation, sp.

Although not an infallible fieldmark, adult males of the eastern box turtle, Terrapene c. carolina, *often have ruby-red irides.*

Stomatitis Mouth infection.

Subspecies The subdivision of a species. A race that may differ slightly in color, size, scalation, or other criteria. Abbreviation, ssp.

Substrate The physical base on which an animal or plant lives.

Sympatric Occurring in the same range without interbreeding.

Taxon (pl. taxa) A classified group of animals or plants.

Taxonomy The science of classification of plants and animals.

Terrestrial Land-dwelling.

Thermoregulate To regulate (body) temperature by choosing a warmer or cooler environment.

Tricarinate Having a triple keel.

Vent The external opening of the cloaca; the anus.

Venter The underside of a creature; the belly.

Ventral Pertaining to the undersurface or belly.

Xeric Characterized by dryness.

Index

Perfect for Pet Owners!

PET OWNER'S MANUALS

Over 50 illustrations per book (20 or more color photos), 72–80 pp., paperback.

ABYSSINIAN CATS
AFRICAN GRAY PARROTS
AMAZON PARROTS
BANTAMS
BEAGLES
BEEKEEPING
BOSTON TERRIERS
BOXERS
CANARIES
CATS
CHINCHILLAS
CHOW-CHOWS
CICHLIDS
COCKATIELS
COCKER SPANIELS
COCKATOOS
COLLIES
CONURES
DACHSHUNDS
DALMATIANS
DISCUS FISH
DOBERMAN PINSCHERS
DOGS
DOVES
DWARF RABBITS
ENGLISH SPRINGER SPANIELS
FEEDING AND SHELTERING BACKYARD
    BIRDS
FEEDING AND SHELTERING EUROPEAN
    BIRDS
FERRETS
GERBILS
GERMAN SHEPHERDS
GOLDEN RETRIEVERS
GOLDFISH
GOULDIAN FINCHES
GREAT DANES
GUINEA PIGS
GUPPIES, MOLLIES, AND PLATTIES
HAMSTERS
HEDGEHOGS
IRISH SETTERS
KEESHONDEN
KILLIFISH
LABRADOR RETRIEVERS
LHASA APSOS
LIZARDS IN THE TERRARIUM
LONGHAIRED CATS

LONG-TAILED PARAKEETS
LORIES AND LORIKEETS
LOVEBIRDS
MACAWS
MICE
MUTTS
MYNAHS
PARAKEETS
PARROTS
PERSIAN CATS
PIGEONS
POMERANIANS
PONIES
POODLES
POT BELLIES AND OTHER MINIATURE PIGS
PUGS
RABBITS
RATS
ROTTWEILERS
SCHNAUZERS
SCOTTISH FOLD CATS
SHAR-PEI
SHEEP
SHETLAND SHEEPDOGS
SHIH TZUS
SIAMESE CATS
SIBERIAN HUSKIES
SMALL DOGS
SNAKES
SPANIELS
TROPICAL FISH
TURTLES
WEST HIGHLAND WHITE TERRIERS
YORKSHIRE TERRIERS
ZEBRA FINCHES

NEW PET HANDBOOKS

Detailed, illustrated profiles (40–60 color photos), 144 pp., paperback.

NEW AQUARIUM FISH HANDBOOK
NEW AUSTRALIAN PARAKEET
    HANDBOOK
NEW BIRD HANDBOOK
NEW CANARY HANDBOOK
NEW CAT HANDBOOK
NEW COCKATIEL HANDBOOK
NEW DOG HANDBOOK
NEW DUCK HANDBOOK
NEW FINCH HANDBOOK

NEW GOAT HANDBOOK
NEW PARAKEET HANDBOOK
NEW PARROT HANDBOOK
NEW RABBIT HANDBOOK
NEW SALTWATER AQUARIUM
    HANDBOOK
NEW SOFTBILL HANDBOOK
NEW TERRIER HANDBOOK

REFERENCE BOOKS

Comprehensive, lavishly illustrated references (60–300 color photos), 136–176 pp., hardcover & paperback.

AQUARIUM FISH
AQUARIUM FISH BREEDING
AQUARIUM FISH SURVIVAL MANUAL
AQUARIUM PLANTS MANUAL
BEFORE YOU BUY THAT PUPPY
BEST PET NAME BOOK EVER, THE
CARING FOR YOUR SICK CAT
CAT CARE MANUAL
CIVILIZING YOUR PUPPY
COMMUNICATING WITH YOUR DOG
COMPLETE BOOK OF BUDGERIGARS
COMPLETE BOOK OF CAT CARE
COMPLETE BOOK OF DOG CARE
DOG CARE MANUAL
FEEDING YOUR PET BIRD
GOLDFISH AND ORNAMENTAL CARP
GUIDE TO A WELL-BEHAVED CAT
GUIDE TO HOME PET GROOMING
HEALTHY CAT, HAPPY CAT
HEALTHY DOG, HAPPY DOG
HOP TO IT: A Guide to Training Your Pet
    Rabbit
HORSE CARE MANUAL
HOW TO TALK TO YOUR CAT
HOW TO TEACH YOUR OLD DOG
    NEW TRICKS
LABYRINTH FISH
NONVENOMOUS SNAKES
TROPICAL MARINE FISH
    SURVIVAL MANUAL

Barron's Educational Series, Inc. • 250 Wireless Blvd., Hauppauge, NY 11788
Call toll-free: 1-800-645-3476 • In Canada: Georgetown Book Warehouse
34 Armstrong Ave., Georgetown, Ont. L7G 4R9 • Call toll-free: 1-800-247-7160
Order from your favorite book or pet store.

(#62) R 2/97